DECEMBER 2023

SUN	MON	TUE	WED	THU	FRI	SAT
					1	2
3	4	5	6	7	8	9
10	11	12	13	14	15	16
17	18	19	20	21	22	23
24	25	26	27	28	29	30
31						

Dear Child Care Professional,

Thanks for choosing the *2024 Redleaf Calendar-Keeper*!

As in years past, this edition of the *Redleaf Calendar-Keeper* contains all the trusted worksheets, expense charts, and tools you rely on to maintain accurate and detailed business records throughout the year. The more information you capture in your *Redleaf Calendar-Keeper*, the more money and time you will save on your taxes.

In addition to all of the record-keeping benefits, a number of great features and items of note are included in this year's *Redleaf Calendar-Keeper*.

Antiracist Themes, Children's Books, and Activities for Young Children
The more opportunities children have to see and share experiences with people of diverse races (including through books like *Eyes That Speak to the Stars*, *Fry Bread: A Native American Family Story*, and *All the Colors We Are*), the less preference they show toward their own race. Along with recommended children's books, throughout the *2024 Redleaf Calendar-Keeper* you will find antiracist activities for children you can easily incorporate into your day. It is never too early to start teaching the value of diversity.

Up-to-Date USDA Reimbursement Guidelines
Every year we research for updates to the United States Department of Agriculture's (USDA's) Child and Adult Care Food Program (CACFP) and integrate any new information so you won't have to worry about identifying the new regulations yourself. Still unsure of ounce equivalents? Go to the Calendar-Keeper web page or RedleafPress.org for easy-to-understand charts.

Literacy Corner
Literacy development starts early in life and is important in developing cognitive skills. The educational and emotional benefits of reading together prepare young children to succeed in school. Each month you will find two suggested children's books that correspond with the month's theme. Many of the 24 children's books, including *All the Colors We Are/Todos los colores de nuestra piel* by Katie Kissinger and *Noah Chases the Wind* by Michelle Worthington, are available at RedleafPress.org/Childrens-Books.

Activities for Children
Ninety percent of brain development occurs by the time a child is five years old. That means those early years are really important! All the inspiration and activities featured in this year's Calendar-Keeper are from Redleaf Press books, including *I Like Myself: Fostering Positive Racial Identity in Young Black Children* by Toni Sturdivant, PhD, and *Loose Parts for Children with Diverse Abilities* by Miriam Beloglovsky. Use these activities to promote healthy brain development and social-emotional learning in the children you care for.

The Experienced Provider
As a child care provider, you have to address many challenges throughout the day. This year's Calendar-Keeper has advice from a variety of Redleaf Press resources, including *Problem Solving with Young Children: Building Creativity, Critical Thinking, and Resilience* by Ann Gadzikowski and *Inclusion Includes Us: Building Bridges and Removing Barriers to Include All Children and Adults in Early Childhood Classrooms* by Mike Huber.

Have a wonderful year!

Your friends at Redleaf Press

Look & Cook Seasonal Menus

Find winter, spring, summer, and autumn seasonal menus for download on the Calendar-Keeper page at **RedleafPress.org/Calendar-Keeper-2024**.

Literacy Corner

Most of the children's books referenced throughout the year in the Literacy Corner are available through Redleaf Press. Grow your children's book library this year.

- *All the Colors We Are/Todos los colores de nuestra piel*
- *Bree Finds a Friend*
- *Noah Chases the Wind*

What Is Think Small Institute?

Our focus is your professional growth.

Our experts know the early childhood field inside and out. They know how to deliver high-quality professional development experiences designed around your needs.

We understand family child care and provide learning opportunities that speak to the unique challenges you face within your family child care program.

What makes Think Small's training stand out?

Through the **Think Small Institute**, we offer eLearning courses across a wide area of topics. Courses are available for clock hour and CEU credit, and you can *learn at your pace—anywhere, anytime.*

Our learning experiences translate evidence-based theory into *practices you can use everyday* in your program. In addition, our courses use an antiracist pedagogy and diversity-inform practice model to *equip you to meet the diverse needs of children and families you serve.*

www.thinksmall.org

Redleaf Press Family Child Care Resources

The Business of Family Child Care: Contracts and Policies
Most family child care providers would rather care for children than write and enforce contracts and policies, but taking care of the children is only part of the job. Contracts and policies are another important part of running a business. This video can help you understand how to establish a good business relationship with the families you serve by creating clear contracts and policies and enforcing them fairly.
#548029-CK24 $49.95

The Business of Family Child Care: Record-Keeping
Most family child care providers would rather care for children than spend time keeping records. But record keeping is an important part of running a business. This training video can help you understand proper record-keeping strategies, help lower taxes, and save family child care providers money.
#547329-CK24 $79.95

The Redleaf Complete Forms Kit
For Both Family Child Care and Center-Based Programs, Revised Edition
Keep your business organized and save hours of time! This CD-ROM includes more than 150 child care forms—the most comprehensive and professionally presented forms available. CD-ROM.
#546520-CK24 $24.95

Infant Daily Report or Toddler Daily Report
Parents fill out the top half of these handy sheets at drop-off, and you report diapering, feeding, napping, and eating information on the bottom half. You'll receive three tablets, each with 60 pages—a six-month supply.
#112101-CK24 $14.95   #112701-CK24 $12.95

Daily Lesson Planner
Schedule your day with this planning aid. It has space to conveniently keep track of activities, learning centers, and more. The planner is on a six-day-per-week cycle. You'll receive three tablets, which are three-hole punched, each with 60 pages—a six-month supply.
#112501-CK24 $14.95

Injury Log
Document injuries on these weekly sheets. Each form is organized with areas to record all relevant information. The tablet is three-hole punched and has 55 forms.
#112301-CK24 $9.95

The Redleaf Family Child Care Curriculum Complete Set
Sharon Woodward

Save almost $20 when you buy the set!
#541080-CK24 $59.95

This starter set includes:

The Redleaf Family Child Care Curriculum, Second Edition
Provide high-quality care with this easy-to-use complete curriculum designed for family child care programs with mixed-age children. 256 pgs.
#544144-CK24 $44.95

The Redleaf Family Child Care Curriculum Developmental Assessment, Revised Edition (10 copies)
Observe and record a child's growth and development with the *Developmental Assessment*.
#544168-CK24 $16.95

The Redleaf Family Child Care Curriculum Family Companion, Revised Edition (10 Copies)
Give families an overview of the *Family Child Care Curriculum*.
#544779-CK24 $10.95

The Redleaf Family Child Care Curriculum Developmental Assessment Guide, Revised Edition
This guide walks you through the process of using the *Developmental Assessment* tool and provides tips to help you communicate with families.
#544786-CK24 $6.95

The Redleaf Family Child Care Curriculum and supplemental materials are available in Spanish! Visit RedleafPress.org for more information (#547177-CK24)

Family Child Care Homes
Creative Spaces for Children to Learn
Linda J. Armstrong

Create warm and inviting places where children feel at home. Loaded with photographs of inventive and practical spaces, you will find inspiration to create your own stimulating and cozy environment. Softbound, 216 pgs.
#540757-CK24 $49.95

The CDA Prep Guide, 4th edition
The Complete Review Manual
Debra Pierce

The up-to-date edition of the easy to understand, *CDA Prep Guide*, offers step-by-step support through the CDA credentialing process and successfully completing the Verification Visit and CDA Exam. Softbound, 232 pgs.
#547244-CK24 $22.95

Save Time and Money Using the Redleaf Calendar-Keeper

2024

For 47 years, the *Redleaf Calendar-Keeper* has saved countless hours of record keeping for family child care providers across the country. It has also helped hundreds of thousands of providers to significantly reduce their taxes.

The *Redleaf Calendar-Keeper* is part of a series of record-keeping resources from Redleaf Press that includes the following titles:

- *Family Child Care Record-Keeping Guide*, **9th edition**: Identifies over 1,000 business deductions
- *Family Child Care Tax Workbook and Organizer*: Use it to do your own taxes
- *Family Child Care Tax Companion*: Use it to educate your tax professional

With these resources, you can keep accurate and detailed records that may mean big tax savings. Here are some important tips for using the *Redleaf Calendar-Keeper* most efficiently.

Three Key Record-Keeping Rules

1. Save receipts for all expenses associated with cleaning, repairing, and maintaining your home.
2. Record all meals served to the children in your care on a daily basis, including all meals not reimbursed by the Food Program.
3. For at least two months, carefully track all the hours you use your home for business, particularly the hours you spend cleaning, preparing activities, and doing other business-related tasks when the children are not present.

How the Redleaf Calendar-Keeper Makes Filing Taxes Easier

Virtually all providers must file IRS Form 1040 Schedule C. It is easier to complete the Schedule C when you keep track of your expenses on the *Redleaf Calendar-Keeper*, which uses the same categories that appear on the Schedule C. In fact, the expenses on the monthly expense report pages are listed in the exact order that they appear on the Schedule C. In addition, we have included five expense categories at the end of the second monthly expense report page: food, toys, household items, cleaning supplies, and activity expenses. These expense categories do not appear directly on the Schedule C, but we've created them to make it easier for you to enter your expenses on the Schedule C. We recommend that you use the series of blank lines under "Other Expenses" on the back of the Schedule C as a place to record these expense categories or other expense categories you have created.

It is important to understand that business expenses can be recorded under any category. For example, children's birthday cards can be recorded under supplies or activity expenses. You can cross out some categories listed in the *Redleaf Calendar-Keeper* and customize the categories for your own use. We left space on these pages to rename a category or to add more categories. In the end, all of your expenses will be totaled on the Schedule C, so you do not need to worry about the placement of an expense in a particular category.

To make it easier to enter expenses under the categories on the *Redleaf Calendar-Keeper* and the Schedule C, we have identified more than 1,000 allowable deductions and their expense categories in the *Family Child Care Record-Keeping Guide*, 9th edition, by Tom Copeland, available from Redleaf Press.

How to Track 100% Business Expenses

It is important that you identify which items are used 100% for business because they are worth more in deductions than items partially used for business. Individual items used 100% for business should be identified as such on the receipt. There are several ways items can be entered in the *Redleaf Calendar-Keeper*. You can write "100%" next to the expense when entering it on the monthly expense report. The 100% items should be added up separately at the end of the year. A Time-Space percentage should be used on all other items in each expense category. For example, let's say you have six items of supplies used 100% for business, totaling $200. Another 25 supply items are used both for business and for your family, totaling $1,000. If your Time-Space percentage is 40%, you can deduct $400 of the shared supplies ($1,000 x 40%) plus the $200 for the 100% business supplies, for a total supplies expense of $600.

Another way to track this on the *Redleaf Calendar-Keeper* is to create two expense categories for supplies. The supplies category already printed on the *Redleaf Calendar-Keeper* could be labeled "100% Supplies." The blank column next to it could be labeled "Shared Supplies." Supplies purchased throughout the year could be listed under the appropriate category. You should claim 100% of the supplies in the first category and the Time-Space percentage of the supplies in the second category. You can eliminate or combine the infrequently used expense categories shown on the calendar in order to have enough space to create the two expense categories that you need for your more frequent expenses.

How to Track Expenses When a Receipt Includes More Than One Expense Category

You can list all of the expenses from one receipt in one category, rather than splitting the receipt between two or more categories. For example, if a receipt has three toy items and two office-expense items, all of the expenses could be listed under either category. Simply decide which category to enter the total expense in and enter it once under that category. A more time-consuming option is to enter the date, check number, store name, and purchase amount for the office expenses on the first monthly expense report page, and the same information again, along with the purchase amount for the toys, on the second monthly expense report page. Either option will work, but remember, it is all added together in the end!

Child and Adult Care Food Program

Money received from the Food Program for children other than your own should be reported as income on your tax form. Money you receive for your own children, if you are income-eligible, is not taxable. Income from the Food Program can be recorded on either the attendance and payment log or the payment and income record. On the attendance and payment log, you can keep a monthly and year-to-date total of Food Program income, parent fees, and other income and still arrive at a year-to-date total income amount. This can help you track your income by category each year.

	FOOD PROGRAM INCOME RECVD	PARENT FEE INCOME RECVD	OTHER INCOME RECVD
FEBRUARY INCOME	$720	$1,500	—
BALANCE FORWARD	$710	$1,400	—
TOTAL Y-T-D INCOME	$1,430	$2,900	—

Using the *Redleaf Calendar-Keeper* with the Standard Meal Allowance Rule

You have two choices for claiming your food expenses. You can keep track of all business and personal food expenses and enter these amounts in the food column on the monthly expense report. Or you can use the standard meal allowance rule, which does not require you to track any food expenses or save any food receipts. For details about claiming food expenses, see the *Family Child Care Record-Keeping Guide*, 9th edition.

To use the standard meal allowance rule, you must maintain records that include the name of each child; the dates and hours of their attendance in care; and the number of breakfasts, lunches, dinners, and snacks served. How you can best use the *Redleaf Calendar-Keeper* to keep these records depends on whether you participate in the Food Program.

IF YOU ARE ON THE FOOD PROGRAM

Your monthly claim form contains all the information you need to track the reimbursed meals you served. Serving sizes for recipes in the *Redleaf Calendar-Keeper* are for ages three to five; adjust your serving according to the children in your care. Save these forms and put the totals on the year-end meal tally on page 95. You can also record the nonreimbursed meals and snacks you served on your monthly claim forms, or you can use the *Redleaf Calendar-Keeper* in one of two ways:

- Track nonreimbursed meals using the meal form on page 94. Photocopy this page, and use one form for each week of the year. You can also download this form at www.redleafpress.org (on the *Redleaf Calendar-Keeper* product page).
- Track nonreimbursed meals using the monthly attendance and payment log. On a separate line for each child, enter the number of nonreimbursed meals served, and total them at the bottom of the form each month.

IF YOU ARE NOT ON THE FOOD PROGRAM

Make sure you fill out the attendance and payment log each month with each child's name and his or her days and hours of attendance.

To track your meals and snacks, use the *Redleaf Calendar-Keeper* in one of two ways:

- Track all your meals and snacks using the meal form on page 94. Photocopy this page, and use one form for each week of the year. You can also download this form at www.redleafpress.org (on the *Redleaf Calendar-Keeper* product page).
- Track all your meals and snacks using the monthly attendance and payment log. On a separate line for each child, enter the number of meals and snacks served, and total them at the bottom of the form each month.

However you track your food expenses, enter the number of reimbursed and nonreimbursed meals on the year-end meal tally on page 95. Fill in the rest of the chart to calculate your food deduction.

How to Use the *Redleaf Calendar-Keeper* to Track Your Hours

There is a place at the top of each month's calendar to record and total the number of hours you care for children and the number of hours you work each month on business-related activities (such as cleaning, planning lessons, preparing meals, keeping records, and so on) when children are not present. A space to fill in your year-to-date total is also provided.

Carefully keeping track of the hours you work in your home will make the biggest difference in reducing your taxes. This is because your work hours are used in a Time-Space calculation that will determine how much of your house expenses you can deduct. These house expenses include your property tax, mortgage interest, utilities, homeowners insurance, house depreciation, house repairs, home improvements, and personal-property depreciation.

HOURS CHILDREN ARE IN YOUR HOME

Record all of the hours children are in your home on the attendance and payment log. You can also track irregular hours in the daily calendar squares. For example:

Leah's normal hours are 7 AM to 5 PM. Total extra hours this week: 16 hours, 45 minutes

SUN	MON	TUE	WED	THU	FRI	SAT
	Quinn leaves 5:30 PM, 30 min.		David arrives 6:45 AM, 15 min.		Ramona stays overnight, arrives 5 PM	Parents pick up Ramona 9 AM, 16 hrs.

CLEANING, COOKING, AND PREPARING ACTIVITIES

The hours you spend preparing for your business when children are not present can be counted in the calculation of the Time-Space percentage. You may record these business hours in one of two ways. The first method is to mark your *Redleaf Calendar-Keeper* each time you are engaged in business activities. The IRS may challenge you by arguing that some of the hours reported were spent in personal activities. To avoid this, record personal activities separately. For example:

SUN	MON	TUE	WED	THU	FRI	SAT
4 PM, business cleaning, 1 hr. 5 PM, personal cleaning, 1 hr. 8 PM, business cooking, 1 hr.	7 PM, business cleaning, 1 hr.		7 AM, business cleaning, 1 hr. 7 PM, personal cleaning, 1 hr.	7 PM, business cooking, 30 min.	7 PM, business cleaning, 1 hr.	8:30 AM, plan trip to park, 30 min.

The second method is to prepare in advance a weekly or monthly schedule that indicates when you plan to spend time on business activities. Such a schedule is likely to be accepted by the IRS if it is kept regularly and followed carefully. You may use the *Redleaf Calendar-Keeper* to prepare your schedule, or you may write it out in a separate notebook. For example:

SUN	MON	TUE	WED	THU	FRI	SAT
1 PM, business cleaning, 1 hr. 2 PM, personal cleaning, 1 hr.	6 AM, business cleaning, 1 hr. 7 PM, personal cleaning, 1 hr.		7 PM, personal cleaning, 1 hr. 8 PM, business cooking, 1 hr.		7 PM, personal cleaning, 1 hr.	

Note: You can detail your plans for one week in the month and let it represent what you will do every week in the month.

PARENT INTERVIEWS AND PHONE CALLS

Record the amount of time you spend outside of regular business hours interviewing parents or talking to parents on the phone.

RECORD KEEPING

Record the time you spend record keeping, planning menus, preparing shopping lists, balancing your checkbook, or doing financial bookkeeping for your business. For example:

SUN	MON	TUE	WED	THU	FRI	SAT
1 — 8 AM, balance checkbook, 30 min.	2	3 — 7 AM, talk to Luca's mother, 15 min.	4	5	6 — 5 PM, interview the Ramoses, 1 hr.	7 — 9 PM, plan menus, 1 hr.
8 — 10 PM, call from Mia's father, Mia is ill, 20 min.	9	10	11	12	13	14 — 9 PM, plan menus, 1 hr.

Notes on Record Keeping

- Review the record-keeping notes on your *Redleaf Calendar-Keeper* at the end of each month to make sure you recorded all your business activities.
- You may not count hours spent away from your home in your Time-Space percentage. This includes time spent shopping or transporting children to school.
- Do not count hours spent on business activities while children are in your care.

For a complete explanation of the Time-Space percentage, refer to chapter 3 of the *Family Child Care Record-Keeping Guide*, 9th edition. (For information about the *Family Child Care Record-Keeping Guide*, 9th edition, see page 66 of the *Redleaf Calendar-Keeper*.)

Attendance and Payment Log

Here are some examples of ways to use the attendance and payment log. Remember, the system to use is the one that works best for you.

EXAMPLE A

Provider has steady attendance, both full-time and part-time child care, but no drop-ins. She is paid whether the child is there or not.

Method 1: Provider enters drop-off and pickup times and records total hours in attendance. Payments are recorded on the payment and income record or on the attendance and payment log. This is the preferred method if you are using the IRS standard meal allowance rate because it shows when children are present.

Method 2: Provider checks (✔) attendance and records total hours in attendance. Parent payments are recorded in the same way as Method 1.

Method 3: Provider writes in total hours in attendance every day and records weekly payment in the TOTAL column of the attendance and payment log.

JANUARY ATTENDANCE AND PAYMENT LOG

CHILD'S NAME	S	M	T	W	T	F	S	TOTAL
Laila		7/5	7/5	7/5	7/5	7/5		50hrs $300

CHILD'S NAME	S	M	T	W	T	F	S	TOTAL
Laila		✔	✔	✔	✔	✔		50hrs $300

CHILD'S NAME	S	M	T	W	T	F	S	TOTAL
Laila		10	10	10	10	10		50hrs $300

EXAMPLE B

Provider does only part-time child care. She is paid by the hour.

Method 1: Provider enters drop-off and pickup times and records total hours in attendance. Payments are recorded on the payment and income record or on the attendance and payment log.

Method 2: Provider uses two lines, noting drop-off and pickup times on the first line, totaling the number of hours in attendance each day on the second line, and recording the total hours in attendance each week in the Saturday column. Payments are recorded in the TOTAL column of the attendance and payment log or on the payment and income record.

CHILD'S NAME	S	M	T	W	T	F	S	TOTAL HRS
Uche			3/5		3/6			5
Gareth		8/10		8/10				4

Uche			3/5		3/6			
			2		3		5	$30
Gareth		8/10		8/10				
		2		2			4	$24

PAYMENT AND INCOME RECORD FOR JANUARY

CHILD'S NAME	JANUARY					JAN TOTAL
	2	8	15	22	29	
Uche	$30					
Gareth	$24					

EXAMPLE C

Provider has a steady full-time child (Laila), a steady part-time child (Gareth), and a drop-in child (Rosie). She uses a combination of methods—Example A, Method 3 (Laila) and Example B, Method 1 (Gareth and Rosie).

CHILD'S NAME	S	M	T	W	T	F	S	TOTAL HRS
Laila		10	10	10	10	10		50
Gareth		8/10		8/10		8/10		6
Rosie			1/4					3

House Expenses Worksheet—see page 84

This chart is designed for recording your utilities and other home expenses. Space is provided for you to record the portion of these expenses that can be claimed as business expenses on your federal income tax return.

Income Tax Worksheet—see page 85

After totaling your expenses for December, enter the yearly amounts on the income tax worksheet. From here you can easily transfer your expenses to the Schedule C.

Payment and Income Record—see pages 86–93

These eight pages for recording your income are an alternative to the attendance and payment log. You can use the attendance and payment log to record attendance only and use the payment and income record to record income. To use these pages, write in the date you expect parents to pay you. In the correct space, record the amount (and the check number) and then the total for the month. At the bottom of the page, include Food Program income and any other income you receive. For the second, third, and fourth quarters, a space is provided for the balance carried forward. A paper clip or piece of tape on the edge of the current payment and income record page will make it easy to find in the *Redleaf Calendar-Keeper*.

PAYMENT AND INCOME RECORD FOR JANUARY

CHILD'S NAME	JANUARY					JAN TOTAL
	2	8	15	22	29	
Uche	4130 $62.00	4229 59.00	4275 89.00	4301 75.00	4362 68.00	353.00
Gareth	Cash 50.00	Cash 50.00	Cash 50.00	Cash 50.00	Cash 50.00	250.00

Emergency Phone Numbers—see pages 96 and 97

Although you should have additional information for each child, this form provides quick access to the basic information. You may want to make a photocopy of this sheet to take with you on outings or field trips. There are lines for your own address and phone number because this information may be needed in an emergency, and you may not be the person making the emergency phone call.

Emergency Drill Record—see page 98

The emergency drill record will help you stay organized and keep an accurate record of this important routine. There is space to record a fire drill and one other emergency drill (for example, storm, tornado, or earthquake) for each month. Faithful practice and good records help keep everyone safe.

Published by Redleaf Press
10 Yorkton Court
St. Paul, MN 55117
www.redleafpress.org

© 2024 by Redleaf Press

All rights reserved. Unless otherwise noted on a specific page, no portion of this publication may be reproduced or transmitted in any form or by any means, electronic or mechanical, including photocopying, recording, or capturing on any information storage and retrieval system, without permission in writing from the publisher, except by a reviewer, who may quote brief passages in a critical article or review to be printed in a magazine or newspaper, or electronically transmitted on radio, television, or the internet.

Forty-seventh edition 2024
Senior editor: Melissa York
Cover design: Renee Hammes
Cover photograph © Adobe Stock
Printed in the United States of America
ISBN 978-1-60554-820-3

Redleaf Press is the publishing division of Think Small.

Please note: Because dates for certain holidays change from year to year, we cannot guarantee their accuracy. Check with your local library if you have questions. The observance of all Jewish and Islamic holidays begins at sundown the previous day.

www.redleafpress.org
800-423-8309

JANUARY 2024

			Hours Worked
	* "No. Hours Open" refers to hours from when the first child arrived to when the last child left (not your advertised work hours).		Previous Total
			No. Hours Open*
	** "Other Hours Worked" refers to hours spent on business activities in the home (cleaning, meal preparation, activity planning, and so on) when children are not present.		Other Hours Worked**
			Year-to-Date Total

SUN	MON	TUE	WED	THU	FRI	SAT
	1 New Year's Day	2 Fire Drill Day Record your vehicle's odometer reading	3	4	5	6
7	8	9	10 Severe Storm Drill Day	11	12	13
14	15 Martin Luther King Jr. Day	16 2023 4th quarter estimated taxes due	17	18	19	20
21	22	23	24	25	26	27
28	29	30	31 Call your local R & R agency; update your service			

Are you ready for tax season? Order your 2023 tax products now!

DECEMBER 2023

S	M	T	W	T	F	S
					1	2
3	4	5	6	7	8	9
10	11	12	13	14	15	16
17	18	19	20	21	22	23
24	25	26	27	28	29	30
31						

FEBRUARY 2024

S	M	T	W	T	F	S
				1	2	3
4	5	6	7	8	9	10
11	12	13	14	15	16	17
18	19	20	21	22	23	24
25	26	27	28	29		

JANUARY

Who Am I?

Today I'm learning all about me,
Who I am now and who I can be!

Recipes

Cottage Cheese and Fruit Bowl

3 cups (1 cup each) kiwi (peeled and sliced), blueberries, and strawberries (sliced)
¾ cup low-fat cottage cheese
6 tablespoons granola (optional)

1. Place kiwi, blueberries, and strawberries in a small bowl. Toss to combine.
2. Place ½ cup fruit each in six bowls. Top with 2 tablespoons cottage cheese and 1 tablespoon granola (optional)

Yield: 6 servings, 1 bowl each
Meal Component: Fruit, Meat/Meat Alternate

Ham and Cheese Pasta Bake

1¼ cups dry whole grain rotini pasta
3 cups marinara sauce
9 ounces diced turkey ham
¾ cup shredded mozzarella cheese

1. Preheat oven to 350° F. Grease a 9 by 9-inch baking dish.
2. In the baking dish, combine all ingredients; mix well. Pasta does not need to be boiled before baking.
3. Bake until hot and bubbling, about 45 minutes.

Yield: About 6 servings, one cup each
Meal Component: Grain, Meat/Meat Alternate

Menu of the Month

Breakfast
Milk
Cottage Cheese and Fruit Bowl*

Morning Snack
Water
Orange Wedges
Almonds

Lunch
Milk
Ham and Cheese Pasta Bake* (WG)
Kiwi
Green Beans

Afternoon Snack
Water
Turkey Slices
Whole Wheat Crackers (WG)

*Indicates recipes of the month.
(WG) Indicates whole grain

Cottage Cheese and Fruit Bowl recipe is adapted from the Institute of Childhood Nutrition.
Ham and Cheese Pasta Bake recipe is adapted from page 101 of *Look & Cook for Family Child Care Homes*.

Nutrition and Fitness Notes

Children grow and develop at different rates. Some children are tall or short for their ages. Some children seem thin, and some seem stout. Children also develop movement skills at different rates. As children's body proportions change, they begin to develop a greater sense of balance. They also gain more control of their large-muscle movements, such as those used in running, jumping, and climbing.

The Experienced Provider

Greet each child by name and give them a warm smile as they arrive. Let them know they are seen and belong here. Your smile acts as a bridge so the child can move from the familiar into the unfamiliar. This seems simple, but in the busyness of the day, these moments can get lost. Make it a priority.

Activities for Children

Measuring Height
Have each child (in a small group) stand up and cut a piece of yarn that is the same height as they are. Then tape each piece in one part of the room, labeled with each child's name. Offer nonstandard measuring tools such as blocks, paperclips, pumpkins, markers, and so on to measure how tall they are and then compare the heights of the others in the classroom. Children can try arranging the yarn from shortest to tallest and then tallest to shortest. Emphasize that people are different in many ways and these differences make life interesting and make us all individuals.

Describing Me
Invite children to create a self-portrait of themselves doing something they love to do. When they have completed their portraits, ask them to choose one word to describe themselves and write it on their artwork (with adult assistance as needed).

Countering Societal Messaging
When thinking about children's multiple identities, we must intentionally plan for those that are marginalized, as they are the identities that are more likely to be left out in adopted curricula or other selected materials. When educators are intentional about countering societal messaging by celebrating and normalizing what was not considered "normal" or celebrated before, we better support children in developing into confident and healthy versions of themselves.

Literacy Corner

Eyes that Speak to the Stars by Joanna Ho
A young boy learns more about who he is and who he will become while learning to love the shape of his eyes, which he shares with his father, grandfather, and baby brother.

Zero by Kathryn Otoshi
Numbers and counting provide a gentle opportunity to discuss body diversity and loving yourself and others along with developing social skills and character.

Serving sizes are for ages 3–5. Guidelines for the proper credit of food may vary in some states. Please check with the CACFP in your state for more information.

JANUARY ATTENDANCE AND PAYMENT LOG

To record drop-off and pickup times that vary, try using two lines per child.

CHILD'S NAME	S 1	M 2	T 3	W 4	T 5	F 6	S	TOTAL	S 7	M 8	T 9	W 10	T 11	F 12	S 13	TOTAL	S 14	M 15	T 16	W 17	T 18	F 19	S 20	TOTAL	S 21	M 22	T 23	W 24	T 25	F 26	S 27	TOTAL	S 28	M 29	T 30	W 31	T	F	S	TOTAL	S	M

JANUARY ATTENDANCE AND PAYMENT LOG CONTINUED

CHILD'S NAME	S	M 1	T 2	W 3	T 4	F 5	S 6	TOTAL	S 7	M 8	T 9	W 10	T 11	F 12	S 13	TOTAL	S 14	M 15	T 16	W 17	T 18	F 19	S 20	TOTAL	S 21	M 22	T 23	W 24	T 25	F 26	S 27	TOTAL	S 28	M 29	T 30	W 31	T	F	S	TOTAL	S	M

WEEKLY PAYMENT TOTALS

	FOOD PROGRAM INCOME RECVD	PARENT FEE INCOME RECVD	OTHER INCOME RECVD			
JANUARY INCOME*				=	JAN TOTAL	
BALANCE FORWARD				=	BALANCE FWD TOTAL	
TOTAL Y-T-D INCOME				=	TOTAL Y-T-D	

Food Program Claim

Date Claim Sent _____

Date Check Received _____

MEAL COUNT TALLY

BREAKFASTS	
LUNCHES	
DINNERS	
SNACKS	

*Include income received in January 2024 for meals served in 2023.

Put totals in year-end meal tally, page 95.

JANUARY EXPENSE REPORT

DATE	PAYMENT TYPE cash, check #, cc #, debit	PURCHASED FROM	PURCHASE TOTAL	ADVERTISING	INSURANCE	INTEREST	LEGAL & PROFESSIONAL SERVICES	OFFICE EXPENSES (including internet & 2nd phone)	RENT OF BUSINESS PROPERTY	REPAIR & MAINTENANCE	SUPPLIES		MILES
		THIS MONTH'S TOTAL											
		BALANCE CARRIED FORWARD											
		YEAR-TO-DATE TOTAL											

JANUARY EXPENSE REPORT

DATE	PAYMENT TYPE cash, check #, cc #, debit	PURCHASED FROM	PURCHASE TOTAL	TAXES & LICENSES	TRAVEL & ENTERTAINMENT	FOOD	TOYS	HOUSEHOLD ITEMS	CLEANING SUPPLIES	ACTIVITY EXPENSES			MILES
		THIS MONTH'S TOTAL											
		BALANCE CARRIED FORWARD											
		YEAR-TO-DATE TOTAL											

See page 85 for an explanation of how to transfer expenses to your tax forms.
You may wish to relabel the columns to fit your business needs.

See page 6 for an explanation of the order in which we present the categories.

FEBRUARY 2024

Hours Worked

| Previous Total |
| No. Hours Open* |
| Other Hours Worked** |
| Year-to-Date Total |

* "No. Hours Open" refers to hours from when the first child arrived to when the last child left (not your advertised work hours).
** "Other Hours Worked" refers to hours spent on business activities in the home (cleaning, meal preparation, activity planning, and so on) when children are not present.

SUN	MON	TUE	WED	THU	FRI	SAT
JANUARY 2024	MARCH 2024			**1** Black History Month / Dental Health Month	**2** Groundhog Day	**3**
4	**5**	**6** Fire Drill Day	**7**	**8**	**9**	**10** Chinese New Year
11	**12**	**13** Mardi Gras	**14** Valentine's Day / Ash Wednesday (Christian) / Severe Storm Drill Day	**15**	**16**	**17**
18	**19** Presidents' Day	**20**	**21**	**22**	**23**	**24**
25	**26**	**27**	**28**	**29** Call your local R & R agency; update your service		

16

FEBRUARY

Imagination Unleashed

We can imagine whatever we choose,
With playful creativity we cannot lose!

Recipes

Hot Chicken Pita Sandwich

3 whole wheat pita bread rounds, at least 1½ ounces each
9 ounces cooked chicken breast, thinly sliced
6 ½-ounce slices mozzarella cheese

1. Preheat oven to 350° F. Line a baking sheet with foil.
2. Slice each pita round in half and open the pocket. Stuff each pocket with 1½ ounces chicken and ½ ounce cheese.
3. Place on baking sheet and heat until cheese melts, about 5 minutes.

Yield: 6 servings, ½ pita round each
Meal Component: Grain, Meat/Meat Alternate

Baked Carrot Fries with Yogurt Dip

¾ cup + 1 tablespoon nonfat plain Greek yogurt
3 tablespoons sunflower seed butter
4 cups baby carrots
1½ teaspoons canola oil

1. For dip: In a small bowl, mix yogurt and sunflower seed butter until smooth. Set aside.
2. For baked carrots: In a small bowl, combine carrots, ⅛ teaspoon salt, and oil. Toss.
3. Place carrots on a baking sheet in a single layer. Bake for 20 minutes at 400° F or until lightly brown on the bottom.

Yield: 6 servings of ½ cup carrot fries (about 6–10) and 2 tablespoons dip
Meal Component: Vegetable, Meat/Meat Alternate

Serving sizes are for ages 3–5. Guidelines for the proper credit of food may vary in some states. Please check with the CACFP in your state for more information.

Menu of the Month

Breakfast
Milk
Scrambled Eggs
Baby Sweet Peppers

Morning Snack
Water
Co-Jack Cheese Cubes
Whole Grain Pretzels (WG)

Lunch
Milk
Hot Chicken Pita Sandwich* (WG)
Apple Slices
Steamed Brussels Sprouts

Afternoon Snack
Water
Baked Carrot Fries with Yogurt Dip*

*Indicates recipes of the month.
(WG) Indicates whole grain

Hot Chicken Pita Sandwich recipe is adapted from page 77 of *Look & Cook for Family Child Care Homes*.
Baked Carrot Fries with Yogurt Dip recipe is adapted from the Institute of Childhood Nutrition.

Nutrition and Fitness Notes

As children learn their own body cues for hunger and fullness, encourage them to communicate when they are full and hungry and to demonstrate their understanding through mealtime serving and eating practices. For most toddlers and preschool children, hunger occurs about every two and a half to three hours. Young children have small stomachs that cannot hold as much food as an adult's can.

The Experienced Provider

Playing with varied, open-ended loose parts nurtures children's critical thinking, inventiveness, creativity, and imagination. Using loose parts in your program fosters essential domains of children's learning and development—social-emotional, language and literacy, cognitive, physical, and creative.

Activities for Children

Try Another Way
Nurture children's creative thinking by inviting them to consider more than one way to solve a problem. Suppose children are playing catch outdoors and their ball gets stuck on a roof. Poking the ball with a stick fails to dislodge the ball. Embrace the problem-solving challenge by saying, "It's time to play Try Another Way. Let's think of a new way to solve this problem." Challenge children further by brainstorming at least three solutions. Some ideas might be silly and impractical, such as "Let's grow some wings and fly up to the roof," but the gamification of the problem-solving process encourages creative thinking and new ideas.

Storytelling with Loose Parts
An array of concrete items such as animals, fairies, trees, and buildings combined with loose parts provides endless creative storytelling opportunities. For children developing decision-making skills or who thrive with fewer choices, limit the pieces to a few of each type. Painting and drawing their own representations on wooden blocks can ignite children's storytelling.

Creatively Building on Strengths
Support children to value their creative spirit and to challenge their thinking about their limitations, including misconceptions about their abilities and capacities. Building on children's strengths instead of focusing only on their needs helps educators recognize that children are creative and capable of imagining positive outcomes.

Literacy Corner

The Year We Learned to Fly by Jacqueline Woodson
At their grandmother's recommendation, a sister and brother learn to use their powerful imaginations to discover new worlds, all while stuck indoors.

Rita and the Firefighters by Mike Huber
Rita wants to join in the imaginative play of her firefighting classmates but has a hard time getting them to listen until her teacher helps the group use their individual imaginations together.

FEBRUARY ATTENDANCE AND PAYMENT LOG

To record drop-off and pickup times that vary, try using two lines per child.

CHILD'S NAME	S	M	T	W	T 1	F 2	S 3	TOTAL	S 4	M 5	T 6	W 7	T 8	F 9	S 10	TOTAL	S 11	M 12	T 13	W 14	T 15	F 16	S 17	TOTAL	S 18	M 19	T 20	W 21	T 22	F 23	S 24	TOTAL	S 25	M 26	T 27	W 28	T 29	F	S	TOTAL	S	M

FEBRUARY ATTENDANCE AND PAYMENT LOG CONTINUED

CHILD'S NAME	S	M	T 1	W 2	T	F 3	S	TOTAL	S 4	M 5	T 6	W 7	T 8	F 9	S 10	TOTAL	S 11	M 12	T 13	W 14	T 15	F 16	S 17	TOTAL	S 18	M 19	T 20	W 21	T 22	F 23	S 24	TOTAL	S 25	M 26	T 27	W 28	T 29	F	S	TOTAL	S	M

WEEKLY PAYMENT TOTALS

	FOOD PROGRAM INCOME RECVD	PARENT FEE INCOME RECVD	OTHER INCOME RECVD			
FEBRUARY INCOME				=	FEB TOTAL	
BALANCE FORWARD				=	BALANCE FWD TOTAL	
TOTAL Y-T-D INCOME				=	TOTAL Y-T-D	

Food Program Claim

Date Claim Sent _____

Date Check Received _____

MEAL COUNT TALLY

BREAKFASTS	
LUNCHES	
DINNERS	
SNACKS	

Put totals in year-end meal tally, page 95.

FEBRUARY EXPENSE REPORT

DATE	PAYMENT TYPE cash, check #, cc #, debit	PURCHASED FROM	PURCHASE TOTAL	ADVERTISING	INSURANCE	INTEREST	LEGAL & PROFESSIONAL SERVICES	OFFICE EXPENSES (including internet & 2nd phone)	RENT OF BUSINESS PROPERTY	REPAIR & MAINTENANCE	SUPPLIES		MILES
		THIS MONTH'S TOTAL											
		BALANCE CARRIED FORWARD											
		YEAR-TO-DATE TOTAL											

FEBRUARY EXPENSE REPORT

DATE	PAYMENT TYPE cash, check #, cc #, debit	PURCHASED FROM	PURCHASE TOTAL	TAXES & LICENSES	TRAVEL & ENTERTAINMENT	FOOD	TOYS	HOUSEHOLD ITEMS	CLEANING SUPPLIES	ACTIVITY EXPENSES			MILES
		THIS MONTH'S TOTAL											
		BALANCE CARRIED FORWARD											
		YEAR-TO-DATE TOTAL											

See page 85 for an explanation of how to transfer expenses to your tax forms.
You may wish to relabel the columns to fit your business needs.

See page 6 for an explanation of the order in which we present the categories.

MARCH 2024

* "No. Hours Open" refers to hours from when the first child arrived to when the last child left (not your advertised work hours).
** "Other Hours Worked" refers to hours spent on business activities in the home (cleaning, meal preparation, activity planning, and so on) when children are not present.

Hours Worked
- Previous Total
- No. Hours Open*
- Other Hours Worked**
- Year-to-Date Total

SUN	MON	TUE	WED	THU	FRI	SAT
					1 National Women's History Month; National Nutrition Month; National Reading Month	**2** Read Across America Day
3	**4**	**5** Fire Drill Day	**6**	**7**	**8**	**9**
10	**11** Ramadan begins (Islamic)	**12**	**13** Severe Storm Drill Day	**14**	**15**	**16**
17 St. Patrick's Day	**18**	**19** Spring begins; Change your smoke alarms and carbon monoxide filter batteries	**20**	**21**	**22**	**23**
24 Palm Sunday (Christian); Purim (Jewish) / **31** Easter Sunday (Christian)	**25**	**26**	**27**	**28**	**29** Good Friday (Christian); Call your local R & R agency; update your service	**30**

MARCH

Our Littlest Ones

Infants and toddlers change every day,
Growing and learning and enjoying play.

Recipes

Banana Pancakes

¾ cup whole wheat flour
1 teaspoon baking powder
⅛ teaspoon salt
1 egg
¾ cup milk
Butter for pan, optional
3 to 3½ cups sliced bananas

1. In a bowl, mix together dry ingredients.
2. In a separate bowl, whisk egg and milk until just mixed. Pour egg mixture into dry ingredients, stirring gently. Batter will be thick.
3. Heat a large skillet over medium heat or set griddle to medium. Add butter, as needed.
4. Pour ¼ cup batter per pancake into pan/griddle. Cook for 30 seconds and then gently press two banana slices into each pancake. Continue cooking until bubbles form on top, about 2–3 minutes.
5. Carefully flip pancakes and cook until browned on the second side, 2–3 more minutes. Hold cooked pancakes in a warm oven until all are cooked.
6. Serve with the remaining bananas.

Yield: 6 servings of one pancake and ½ cup bananas
Meal Component: Grain, Fruit

Whipped Sweet Potatoes

14 ounces sweet potatoes, fresh, peeled, cut into quarters (about 3⅛ cups)
1 tablespoon 1% low-fat milk
1 tablespoon margarine

Menu of the Month

Breakfast
Milk
Banana Pancakes* (WG)

Morning Snack
Water
Grapes
Hard-Boiled Eggs

Lunch
Milk
Grilled Chicken
Whipped Sweet Potatoes*
Melon Balls
Whole Wheat Roll (WG)

Afternoon Snack
Water
Celery Sticks
Peanut Butter

*Indicates recipes of the month.
(WG) Indicates whole grain

Banana Pancakes recipe is adapted from pages 37–38 of *Look & Cook for Family Child Care Homes*.
Whipped Sweet Potatoes recipe is adapted from the US Department of Agriculture.

1. Place sweet potatoes in a pot of water, and bring to a boil. Cook until fork tender, about 20 minutes. Drain well.
2. In a medium bowl, immediately combine drained sweet potatoes, milk, margarine, and salt and pepper to taste.
3. Using an electric mixer, mix on medium speed until potatoes are smooth and fluffy.

Yield: 6 ¼-cup servings
Meal Component: Vegetable

Nutrition and Fitness Notes

Be breast-feeding friendly. Provide a private nook or room to make breast-feeding more comfortable and follow a feeding schedule that accommodates families' needs. Follow current Centers for Disease Control recommendations for storage and feeding: www.cdc.gov/breastfeeding/recommendations/handling_breastmilk.htm.

The Experienced Provider

No matter how many years we've been educating and caring for children, there are always new situations and new challenges. In early childhood especially, children grow and develop new skills, abilities, interests, and curiosities at a rapid pace, which means that group dynamics are constantly changing and evolving. Each step forward in learning presents new challenges.

Activities for Children

Mirror Play

Use moments when infants are enjoying their reflections in a mirror to talk about skin tone and hair texture and color in a positive way. We often point out other things, like the colors of their onesies or the smiles on their faces. We can use this same approach to say uplifting words about the many shades of skin and textures of hair found in the room.

Home Visits

When possible, make home visits. Listening and asking questions will help you learn from the family. Visits also help the family feel included and valued. Prepare a bag with infant-safe loose parts to give to the families and include a handout in families' home language about how the loose parts support children's learning, stimulate creativity, and engage the brain. Loose parts are also less expensive than many commercial toys, making them easier for families to incorporate into everyday play activities.

Messages for Infants

Because we know that infants attend to racial differences, we must start sending our youngest learners positive messages about human diversity. In an infant classroom, we have the power to spread positivity perhaps before negative messaging has become internalized. What an honor!

Literacy Corner

Littles: and How They Grow by Kelly DiPucchio
This simple rhyming celebration of babies features adorable illustrations of multicultural littles.

All the Colors We Are by Katie Kissinger
Filled with photographs of children of all skin tones, *All the Colors We Are* provides a simple and engaging explanation of how each person's skin color is determined by ancestors, the sun, and melanin.

Serving sizes are for ages 3–5. Guidelines for the proper credit of food may vary in some states. Please check with the CACFP in your state for more information.

MARCH ATTENDANCE AND PAYMENT LOG

To record drop-off and pickup times that vary, try using two lines per child.

CHILD'S NAME	S	M	T	W	T	F 1	S 2	TOTAL	S 3	M 4	T 5	W 6	T 7	F 8	S 9	TOTAL	S 10	M 11	T 12	W 13	T 14	F 15	S 16	TOTAL	S 17	M 18	T 19	W 20	T 21	F 22	S 23	TOTAL	S 24	M 25	T 26	W 27	T 28	F 29	S 30	TOTAL	S 31	M

MARCH ATTENDANCE AND PAYMENT LOG CONTINUED

WEEKLY PAYMENT TOTALS

CHILD'S NAME	S 1	M 2	T	W	T	F	S	TOTAL	S	M	T	W	T	F	S 9	TOTAL	S 10	M 11	T 12	W 13	T 14	F 15	S 16	TOTAL	S 17	M 18	T 19	W 20	T 21	F 22	S 23	TOTAL	S 24	M 25	T 26	W 27	T 28	F 29	S 30	TOTAL	M 31	S

MARCH INCOME

FOOD PROGRAM INCOME REC'D	PARENT FEE INCOME REC'D	OTHER INCOME REC'D		
			=	MAR TOTAL
			=	BALANCE FWD TOTAL
			=	TOTAL Y-T-D

BALANCE FORWARD

TOTAL Y-T-D INCOME

Food Program Claim

Date Claim Sent _____

Date Check Received _____

MEAL COUNT TALLY

BREAKFASTS	
LUNCHES	
DINNERS	
SNACKS	

Put totals in year-end meal tally, page 95.   25

MARCH EXPENSE REPORT

DATE	PAYMENT TYPE cash, check #, cc #, debit	PURCHASED FROM	PURCHASE TOTAL	ADVERTISING	INSURANCE	INTEREST	LEGAL & PROFESSIONAL SERVICES	OFFICE EXPENSES (including internet & 2nd phone)	RENT OF BUSINESS PROPERTY	REPAIR & MAINTENANCE	SUPPLIES		MILES
			THIS MONTH'S TOTAL										
			BALANCE CARRIED FORWARD										
			YEAR-TO-DATE TOTAL										

MARCH EXPENSE REPORT

DATE	PAYMENT TYPE cash, check #, cc #, debit	PURCHASED FROM	PURCHASE TOTAL	TAXES & LICENSES	TRAVEL & ENTERTAINMENT	FOOD	TOYS	HOUSEHOLD ITEMS	CLEANING SUPPLIES	ACTIVITY EXPENSES			MILES
		THIS MONTH'S TOTAL											
		BALANCE CARRIED FORWARD											
		YEAR-TO-DATE TOTAL											

See page 85 for an explanation of how to transfer expenses to your tax forms. You may wish to relabel the columns to fit your business needs.

See page 6 for an explanation of the order in which we present the categories.

APRIL 2024

	Hours Worked
	Previous Total
	No. Hours Open*
	Other Hours Worked**
	Year-to-Date Total

* "No. Hours Open" refers to hours from when the first child arrived to when the last child left (not your advertised work hours).
** "Other Hours Worked" refers to hours spent on business activities in the home (cleaning, meal preparation, activity planning, and so on) when children are not present.

SUN	MON	TUE	WED	THU	FRI	SAT
	1 April Fools' Day National Child Abuse Prevention Month Fire Drill Day	**2**	**3**	**4**	**5**	**6**
7	**8** Week of the Young Child	**9** Ramadan ends (Islamic)	**10** Eid al-Fitr (Islamic) National Siblings Day Severe Storm Drill Day	**11**	**12**	**13**
14	**15** Patriots' Day 2023 income taxes due 2024 1st quarter estimated taxes due	**16**	**17**	**18**	**19**	**20**
21	**22** Earth Day	**23** Passover begins (Jewish)	**24**	**25**	**26** Arbor Day	**27**
28	**29**	**30** Passover ends (Jewish) Call your local R & R agency; update your service				

MARCH 2024

S	M	T	W	T	F	S
					1	2
3	4	5	6	7	8	9
10	11	12	13	14	15	16
17	18	19	20	21	22	23
24	25	26	27	28	29	30
31						

MAY 2024

S	M	T	W	T	F	S
			1	2	3	4
5	6	7	8	9	10	11
12	13	14	15	16	17	18
19	20	21	22	23	24	25
26	27	28	29	30	31	

APRIL

The Great Outdoors
Outdoors is the place to be,
Out in the sun we feel so free!

Recipes

English Muffin Egg Sandwich

6 eggs
3 whole wheat English muffins, at least 1 ounce each, split into 6 rounds
6 ounces turkey ham
⅜ cup shredded cheddar cheese

1. Preheat oven to 350° F. Grease a 6-cup muffin pan or 6 ramekins and place on a baking sheet.
2. Crack one egg into each cup or ramekin. Beat slightly. Season with salt and pepper.
3. Bake eggs until set, about 10–15 minutes. Meanwhile, toast the English muffins.
4. Remove eggs from oven and allow to cool slightly. To remove egg, run a knife around the edge.
5. Top each English muffin with 1 ounce turkey ham, 1 egg, and 1 tablespoon cheese.

Yield: 6 servings, one sandwich each
Meal Component: Grain, Meat/Meat Alternate

Cheesy Baked Broccoli Bites

4 cups frozen broccoli florets
1 cup shredded cheddar cheese
1 large egg
2 tablespoons water
½ cup plain bread crumbs

1. Preheat oven to 350° F. Line a baking sheet with foil.
2. Cook broccoli according to package directions. Allow broccoli to cool, then place in a colander lined with paper towels and squeeze out the excess moisture.
3. In a bowl, whisk the egg and water. Mix the bread crumbs and cheese in a separate bowl.
4. Dip the broccoli in the egg wash and then into the bread crumb mixture and place on the baking sheet.
5. Bake until golden brown, about 10–15 minutes.

Yield: 6 servings, ⅔ cup per serving
Meal Component: Vegetable, Meat/Meat Alternate

Menu of the Month

Breakfast
Milk
English Muffin Egg Sandwich* (WG)
Mixed Berries

Morning Snack
Water
Pineapple
Mini Whole Grain Waffles (WG)

Lunch
Milk
Hamburgers on Whole Wheat Buns (WG)
Baby Carrots
Canned Fruit Cocktail

Afternoon Snack
Water
Cheesy Baked Broccoli Bites*

*Indicates recipes of the month.
(WG) Indicates whole grain
English Muffin Egg Sandwich recipe is adapted from page 47 of *Look & Cook for Family Child Care Homes*.
Cheesy Baked Broccoli Bites recipe can be found on page 164 of *Look & Cook for Family Child Care Homes*.

Nutrition and Fitness Notes

Physical activity does not require expensive equipment or a highly structured exercise program. Large open areas provide opportunities for running, jumping, and rolling. Parachute activities promote coordination and cooperation. Walking on a wooden board placed on the ground promotes balance and coordination. Nature walks are a fun way to be physically active while integrating discovery and science activities.

The Experienced Provider

Our ethical responsibilities as early childhood educators call us to prioritize children's safety. We must protect children from hazards, but we must allow children to experience risk. Ask questions to empower the child to become more focused on what they're doing, like "Do you feel safe?" and "Do you feel strong and ready to do this?"

Activities for Children

Nature Walk
Many books about human skin color differences describe shades of brown with beautiful descriptive language. Extend a read aloud about the shades of human skin to include celebrating brown in other parts of nature. Take children on a nature walk to look for different shades of brown. Children can write or draw their observations and share them with others.

Rough-and-Tumble
In rough-and-tumble play, children climb over one another, wrestle, roll around, and even pretend to fight. This type of play is a basic human instinct that helps children develop many skills. Simple changes in the environment increase safety for this type of play. Add ropes so children can engage in tug-of-war. Rolled-up newspapers made into long "swords" allow children to fence with one another. Setting mats outdoors invites children to roll or wrestle.

Belonging
What can you do so every child feels they belong? Rather than focus on how to make the child fit in to the program culture, we need to create a culture that fits all children. Take a look at the learning environment, both physical and emotional, and ask, "What are the barriers preventing a child from engaging in the community?"

Literacy Corner

Run Wild by David Covell
Messy and vibrant illustrations accompany this rhyming story that follows childhood adventures in the great outdoors.

Noah Chases the Wind by Michelle Worthington
Noah's inquisitive nature takes him on an adventure to answer the question, "Where does the wind go?"

Serving sizes are for ages 3–5. Guidelines for the proper credit of food may vary in some states. Please check with the CACFP in your state for more information.

APRIL ATTENDANCE AND PAYMENT LOG

To record drop-off and pickup times that vary, try using two lines per child.

CHILD'S NAME	S	M 1	T 2	W 3	T 4	F 5	S 6	TOTAL	S 7	M 8	T 9	W 10	T 11	F 12	S 13	TOTAL	S 14	M 15	T 16	W 17	T 18	F 19	S 20	TOTAL	S 21	M 22	T 23	W 24	T 25	F 26	S 27	TOTAL	S 28	M 29	T 30	W	T	F	S	TOTAL	S	M

APRIL ATTENDANCE AND PAYMENT LOG CONTINUED

CHILD'S NAME	S	M 1	T 2	W 3	T 4	F 5	S 6	TOTAL	S 7	M 8	T 9	W 10	T 11	F 12	S 13	TOTAL	S 14	M 15	T 16	W 17	T 18	F 19	S 20	TOTAL	S 21	M 22	T 23	W 24	T 25	F 26	S 27	TOTAL	S 28	M 29	T 30	W	T	F	S	TOTAL	S	M		

WEEKLY PAYMENT TOTALS

	FOOD PROGRAM INCOME RECVD	PARENT FEE INCOME RECVD	OTHER INCOME RECVD			
APRIL INCOME				=	APR TOTAL	
BALANCE FORWARD				=	BALANCE FWD TOTAL	
TOTAL Y-T-D INCOME				=	TOTAL Y-T-D	

Food Program Claim

Date Claim Sent _____

Date Check Received _____

MEAL COUNT TALLY

BREAKFASTS	
LUNCHES	
DINNERS	
SNACKS	

Put totals in year-end meal tally, page 95.

APRIL EXPENSE REPORT

DATE	PAYMENT TYPE cash, check #, cc #, debit	PURCHASED FROM	PURCHASE TOTAL	ADVERTISING	INSURANCE	INTEREST	LEGAL & PROFESSIONAL SERVICES	OFFICE EXPENSES (including internet & 2nd phone)	RENT OF BUSINESS PROPERTY	REPAIR & MAINTENANCE	SUPPLIES		MILES
		THIS MONTH'S TOTAL											
		BALANCE CARRIED FORWARD											
		YEAR-TO-DATE TOTAL											

APRIL EXPENSE REPORT

DATE	PAYMENT TYPE cash, check #, cc #, debit	PURCHASED FROM	PURCHASE TOTAL	TAXES & LICENSES	TRAVEL & ENTERTAINMENT	FOOD	TOYS	HOUSEHOLD ITEMS	CLEANING SUPPLIES	ACTIVITY EXPENSES			MILES
		THIS MONTH'S TOTAL											
		BALANCE CARRIED FORWARD											
		YEAR-TO-DATE TOTAL											

See page 85 for an explanation of how to transfer expenses to your tax forms.
You may wish to relabel the columns to fit your business needs.

See page 6 for an explanation of the order in which we present the categories.

MAY 2024

	Hours Worked
	Previous Total
	No. Hours Open*
	Other Hours Worked**
	Year-to-Date Total

* "No. Hours Open" refers to hours from when the first child arrived to when the last child left (not your advertised work hours).
** "Other Hours Worked" refers to hours spent on business activities in the home (cleaning, meal preparation, activity planning, and so on) when children are not present.

SUN	MON	TUE	WED	THU	FRI	SAT
APRIL 2024 / JUNE 2024 reference calendars			**1** Physical Fitness and Sports Month; May Day	**2**	**3**	**4**
5 Orthodox Easter (Orthodox); Cinco de Mayo	**6** Fire Drill Day	**7** National Teacher Day	**8** Severe Storm Drill Day	**9**	**10** Provider Appreciation Day	**11**
12 Mother's Day	**13**	**14**	**15**	**16**	**17**	**18**
19 Pentecost (Christian)	**20**	**21**	**22**	**23**	**24**	**25** National Missing Children's Day
26	**27** Memorial Day	**28**	**29**	**30**	**31** Call your local R & R agency; update your service	

MAY

Loose Parts Everywhere
With seashells, and acorns, and bottle caps galore,
We love loose parts more and more!

Recipes

Strawberry and Waffle Kebabs
¾ cup nonfat vanilla Greek yogurt
1 tablespoon maple syrup
3 whole grain frozen waffles, at least 1.2 ounces each
36 whole strawberries, at least 3 cups

1. Gather 12 sticks for kebabs.
2. In a small bowl, whisk yogurt and maple syrup until well-blended.
3. Lightly toast waffles for 3–4 minutes. Cut each waffle into 4 triangles.
4. Build kebabs with 3 strawberries and 1 waffle triangle each.

Yield: 6 servings of 2 kebabs and ⅛ cup maple-yogurt dip
Meal Component: Fruit, Grain

Spinach Salad
5 large hard-boiled eggs
1 tablespoon extra virgin olive oil
2 tablespoons raspberry vinegar
1 tablespoon pasteurized honey
3 cups baby spinach
¾ cup dried cranberries
2 tablespoons unsalted sunflower seeds
1 teaspoon grated Parmesan cheese

1. Peel eggs (if necessary). Cut into quarters. Set aside.
2. To make salad dressing: In a small bowl, combine oil, vinegar, and honey with salt to taste. Whisk to blend.
3. In a large bowl, combine spinach, cranberries, and sunflower seeds. Add dressing. Toss. Sprinkle with Parmesan cheese.

Yield: 6 servings of ⅔ cup salad with 3 egg quarters
Meal Component: Vegetable, Fruit, Meat/Meat Alternate

Menu of the Month

Breakfast
Milk
Strawberry and Waffle Kebabs* (WG)

Morning Snack
Water
Cucumber Slices
Mini Whole-Grain Bagels (WG)

Lunch
Milk
Spinach Salad*
Whole Grain Toast (WG)

Afternoon Snack
Water
Bananas
Sunflower Butter

*Indicates recipes of the month.
(WG) Indicates whole grain
Strawberry and Waffle Kebabs recipe is adapted from the Institute of Childhood Nutrition.
Spinach Salad recipe is adapted from the Institute of Childhood Nutrition.

Nutrition and Fitness Notes

Encourage a homelike environment by involving children in passing serving bowls and serving themselves. Occasionally use place mats, tablecloths, centerpieces, and cloth napkins to make the table setting attractive and to show children a variety of table settings.

The Experienced Provider

If children are not engaging with specific loose parts, consider why not. Perhaps items need to be more visible, in a different play space, paired with an appropriate accessory, or displayed with visual appeal. Think about changes you could make to increase interest.

Activities for Children

Loose Parts for Constructing
Provide a variety of Loose Parts for designing, engineering, and constructing. Moving loose parts into different areas helps children explore varied possibilities. Rocks balance differently on a smooth surface than on grass, for example. Combining different loose parts increases interest and engagement. Cardboard tubes combined with wooden blocks challenge children to build with both flat and round surfaces.

Hair Accessories
Celebrate Afro-textured hair to counter negative messaging. Black hairstyles use so many hair accessories: beads, bows, ribbons, barrettes, small hair ties, clips, beaded ponytail holders, headbands, and more. Any of these items can be counted, sorted by color, lined up by size, and so on. Choose items that are large enough to not be a choking hazard.

Seeing Ourselves in Play
To support the whole child, we must help them build their sense of self and identity. Take photos of children engaged in active exploration and mount them on small blocks or CD cases so they can represent themselves in their play. The photo blocks invite children to engage in powerful conversations about differences and similarities.

Literacy Corner

The Most Magnificent Thing by Ashley Spires
Being a creator is hard, and often there are many setbacks before the vision is realized. A little break with a friend can help us push forward, sometimes toward a new dream!

Kimmy's Marvelous Wind-Catching Wonder by Linda Glaser
Kimmy spends all morning with ribbons, paper, scissors, and glue as she builds her very own kite. Will it fly?

Serving sizes are for ages 3–5. Guidelines for the proper credit of food may vary in some states. Please check with the CACFP in your state for more information.

MAY ATTENDANCE AND PAYMENT LOG

To record drop-off and pickup times that vary, try using two lines per child.

CHILD'S NAME	S	M	T 1	W 2	T 3	F 4	S	TOTAL	S 5	M 6	T 7	W 8	T 9	F 10	S 11	TOTAL	S 12	M 13	T 14	W 15	T 16	F 17	S 18	TOTAL	S 19	M 20	T 21	W 22	T 23	F 24	S 25	TOTAL	S 26	M 27	T 28	W 29	T 30	F 31	S	TOTAL	S	M	

MAY ATTENDANCE AND PAYMENT LOG CONTINUED

CHILD'S NAME	S	M	T	W 1	T 2	F 3	S 4	TOTAL	S 5	M 6	T 7	W 8	T 9	F 10	S 11	TOTAL	S 12	M 13	T 14	W 15	T 16	F 17	S 18	TOTAL	S 19	M 20	T 21	W 22	T 23	F 24	S 25	TOTAL	S 26	M 27	T 28	W 29	T 30	F 31	TOTAL	S	M
WEEKLY PAYMENT TOTALS																																									

	FOOD PROGRAM INCOME RECVD	PARENT FEE INCOME RECVD	OTHER INCOME RECVD			
MAY INCOME				=	MAY TOTAL	
BALANCE FORWARD				=	BALANCE FWD TOTAL	
TOTAL Y-T-D INCOME				=	TOTAL Y-T-D	

Food Program Claim

Date Claim Sent _____

Date Check Received _____

MEAL COUNT TALLY

BREAKFASTS	
LUNCHES	
DINNERS	
SNACKS	

Put totals in year-end meal tally, page 95.

MAY EXPENSE REPORT

DATE	PAYMENT TYPE cash, check #, cc #, debit	PURCHASED FROM	PURCHASE TOTAL	ADVERTISING	INSURANCE	INTEREST	LEGAL & PROFESSIONAL SERVICES	OFFICE EXPENSES (including internet & 2nd phone)	RENT OF BUSINESS PROPERTY	REPAIR & MAINTENANCE	SUPPLIES		MILES
		THIS MONTH'S TOTAL											
		BALANCE CARRIED FORWARD											
		YEAR-TO-DATE TOTAL											

MAY EXPENSE REPORT

DATE	PAYMENT TYPE cash, check #, cc #, debit	PURCHASED FROM	PURCHASE TOTAL	TAXES & LICENSES	TRAVEL & ENTERTAINMENT	FOOD	TOYS	HOUSEHOLD ITEMS	CLEANING SUPPLIES	ACTIVITY EXPENSES			MILES
		THIS MONTH'S TOTAL											
		BALANCE CARRIED FORWARD											
		YEAR-TO-DATE TOTAL											

See page 85 for an explanation of how to transfer expenses to your tax forms.
You may wish to relabel the columns to fit your business needs.

See page 6 for an explanation of the order in which we present the categories.

JUNE 2024

Hours Worked	
Previous Total	
No. Hours Open*	
Other Hours Worked**	
Year-to-Date Total	

* "No. Hours Open" refers to hours from when the first child arrived to when the last child left (not your advertised work hours).

** "Other Hours Worked" refers to hours spent on business activities in the home (cleaning, meal preparation, activity planning, and so on) when children are not present.

Replenish your stock of Family Child Care Business Receipt Books, Inventory-Keepers, and Mileage-Keepers.

SUN	MON	TUE	WED	THU	FRI	SAT
						1
2	**3** Fire Drill Day	**4**	**5**	**6**	**7**	**8**
9	**10**	**11**	**12** Shavuot (Jewish) / Severe Storm Drill Day	**13**	**14** Hajj begins (Islamic) / Flag Day	**15**
16 Father's Day	**17** Eid al-Adha begins (Islamic) / 2024 2nd quarter estimated taxes due	**18**	**19** Juneteenth	**20** Summer begins	**21**	**22**
23 / **30**	**24**	**25**	**26**	**27**	**28** Call your local R & R agency; update your service	**29**

MAY 2024

S	M	T	W	T	F	S
			1	2	3	4
5	6	7	8	9	10	11
12	13	14	15	16	17	18
19	20	21	22	23	24	25
26	27	28	29	30	31	

JULY 2024

S	M	T	W	T	F	S
	1	2	3	4	5	6
7	8	9	10	11	12	13
14	15	16	17	18	19	20
21	22	23	24	25	26	27
28	29	30	31			

JUNE

Showing We Care
Playing and laughing and learning to share,
These are all ways we show how we care.

Recipes

Sautéed Tempeh with Vegetables
1½ cups fresh cauliflower
1 teaspoon vegetable oil
9 oz plain tempeh
6 tablespoons teriyaki sauce
1 teaspoon garlic powder
1 tablespoon minced dehydrated onion
1¼ cups baby spinach

1. Make cauliflower rice: Wash cauliflower and grate or cut into very small, rice-sized pieces. Set aside.
2. Heat oil on medium-high heat in a medium sauté pan. Break tempeh into crumbles. Cook for 5–7 minutes or until it starts to turn golden brown. Stir frequently.
3. Reduce heat to medium. Add teriyaki sauce. Cook until sauce begins to thicken and caramelize. Stir frequently.
4. Add cauliflower rice, garlic powder, and dehydrated onion. Cook for 2 minutes. Stir frequently.
5. Add baby spinach. Stir constantly until spinach is completely wilted, about 2–3 minutes.

Yield: 6 ⅓-cup servings
Meal Component: Vegetables, Meat/Meat Alternate

Corn Salad
1 cup diced fresh tomatoes
1 cup whole kernel corn, cooked and cooled
1 cup canned black beans, rinsed and drained
1 teaspoon taco seasoning mix (low sodium)

Menu of the Month

Breakfast
Milk
Whole Grain Cereal (WG)
Blueberries

Morning Snack
Water
String Cheese
Peas in the Pod

Lunch
Milk
Sautéed Tempeh with Vegetables*
Whole Grain Breadstick (WG)
Plum Slices

Afternoon Snack
Water
Corn Salsa*

*Indicates recipes of the month.
(WG) Indicates whole grain
Sautéed Tempeh with Vegetables recipe is adapted from the Institute of Childhood Nutrition.
Corn Salsa recipe is adapted from page 153 of *Look & Cook for Family Child Care Homes*.

1. Mix all ingredients together.

Yield: 6 ½-cup servings
Meal Component: Vegetable

Nutrition and Fitness Notes

Mealtime and snacktime activities provide opportunities to show children how to share food appropriately. Show children how to cut a sandwich in half before taking a bite, how to pour beverages from a small pitcher into individual cups, and how to use tongs or a napkin to remove a cracker or cookie from a serving tray.

The Experienced Provider

Rituals create community. They create a togetherness that brings about the confidence to be yourself. This confidence enables children to try new experiences and to share ideas and feelings without the fear of being embarrassed. The community holds them in a nest of security, allowing them to explore, experiment, and adventure. What rituals have you incorporated in your program?

Activities for Children

Getting to Know You
The most important word in the world is your name! Sing songs that include children's names, like "Hickety Tickety Bumble Bee" and "Willoughby Wallaby Woo." Write each child's name on a card to spark curiosity about letters and words. Play games with names, and sort them into different groups, such as beginning or final letters, number of letters, and so on.

How Do You Say Hello?
Ask families to tell you one way that they might greet a close friend or relative that is not hello. Make a book featuring pictures of each child with their family's chosen greeting(s) on the opposite page. A small photo album makes a great base for this book.

Authentic Representation
As you plan to create inclusive and culturally responsive environments, ensure that every child is represented in an authentic and respectful way. The focus must be on children's individual strengths as well as the strengths of the combined ecosystem. Be sure to include imagery that represents cultures not present in the community too.

Literacy Corner

Bree Finds a Friend by Mike Huber
Bree enjoys digging up earthworms solo until another friend joins her playtime activity.

Just Ask!: Be Different, Be Brave, Be You by Sonia Sotomayor
Just Ask! empowers children with varying differences in abilities to share their strengths and unique qualities, celebrating how each one of us brings something better into the world.

JUNE ATTENDANCE AND PAYMENT LOG

To record drop-off and pickup times that vary, try using two lines per child.

CHILD'S NAME	S 1	M	T	W	T	F	S	TOTAL	S 2	M 3	T 4	W 5	T 6	F 7	S 8	TOTAL	S 9	M 10	T 11	W 12	T 13	F 14	S 15	TOTAL	S 16	M 17	T 18	W 19	T 20	F 21	S 22	TOTAL	S 23	M 24	T 25	W 26	T 27	F 28	S 29	TOTAL	S 30	M

JUNE ATTENDANCE AND PAYMENT LOG CONTINUED

CHILD'S NAME	S	M	T	W	T	F	S 1	TOTAL	S 2	M 3	T 4	W 5	T 6	F 7	S 8	TOTAL	S 9	M 10	T 11	W 12	T 13	F 14	S 15	TOTAL	S 16	M 17	T 18	W 19	T 20	F 21	S 22	TOTAL	S 23	M 24	T 25	W 26	T 27	F 28	S 29	TOTAL	S 30	M
WEEKLY PAYMENT TOTALS																																											

	FOOD PROGRAM INCOME RECVD	PARENT FEE INCOME RECVD	OTHER INCOME RECVD			
JUNE INCOME				=	JUN TOTAL	
BALANCE FORWARD				=	BALANCE FWD TOTAL	
TOTAL Y-T-D INCOME				=	TOTAL Y-T-D	

Food Program Claim

Date Claim Sent _____

Date Check Received _____

MEAL COUNT TALLY

BREAKFASTS	
LUNCHES	
DINNERS	
SNACKS	

Put totals in year-end meal tally, page 95.

JUNE EXPENSE REPORT

DATE	PAYMENT TYPE cash, check #, cc #, debit	PURCHASED FROM	PURCHASE TOTAL	ADVERTISING	INSURANCE	INTEREST	LEGAL & PROFESSIONAL SERVICES	OFFICE EXPENSES (including internet & 2nd phone)	RENT OF BUSINESS PROPERTY	REPAIR & MAINTENANCE	SUPPLIES		MILES
		THIS MONTH'S TOTAL											
		BALANCE CARRIED FORWARD											
		YEAR-TO-DATE TOTAL											

JUNE EXPENSE REPORT

DATE	PAYMENT TYPE cash, check #, cc #, debit	PURCHASED FROM	PURCHASE TOTAL	TAXES & LICENSES	TRAVEL & ENTERTAINMENT	FOOD	TOYS	HOUSEHOLD ITEMS	CLEANING SUPPLIES	ACTIVITY EXPENSES			MILES
		THIS MONTH'S TOTAL											
		BALANCE CARRIED FORWARD											
		YEAR-TO-DATE TOTAL											

See page 85 for an explanation of how to transfer expenses to your tax forms. You may wish to relabel the columns to fit your business needs.

See page 6 for an explanation of the order in which we present the categories.

JULY 2024

	Hours Worked
	Previous Total
No. Hours Open*	
Other Hours Worked**	
Year-to-Date Total	

* "No. Hours Open" refers to hours from when the first child arrived to when the last child left (not your advertised work hours).
** "Other Hours Worked" refers to hours spent on business activities in the home (cleaning, meal preparation, activity planning, and so on) when children are not present.

SUN	MON	TUE	WED	THU	FRI	SAT
	1 Fire Drill Day	2	3	4 Independence Day	5	6
7 Islamic New Year	8	9	10 Severe Storm Drill Day	11	12	13
14	15	16	17 Ashura (Islamic)	18	19	20
21	22	23	24	25	26	27
28 Parents' Day	29	30 Friendship Day	31 Call your local R & R agency; update your service			

JUNE 2024

S	M	T	W	T	F	S
						1
2	3	4	5	6	7	8
9	10	11	12	13	14	15
16	17	18	19	20	21	22
23	24	25	26	27	28	29
30						

AUGUST 2024

S	M	T	W	T	F	S
				1	2	3
4	5	6	7	8	9	10
11	12	13	14	15	16	17
18	19	20	21	22	23	24
25	26	27	28	29	30	31

JULY

Trying New Foods
There are so many new foods to eat,
Try something savory and something sweet!

Recipes

Baked Tilapia
¼ cup whole-wheat, seasoned breadcrumbs
1 teaspoon herbs de Provence seasoning blend
13½ oz tilapia fish fillets, fresh or thawed if frozen (each piece should be about 2¼ oz)
4 teaspoons reduced-fat mayonnaise

1. Preheat oven to 400° F. Place a baking rack on top of a baking sheet. Spray rack with nonstick cooking spray. Set aside.
2. In a small bowl, combine breadcrumbs and herbs de Provence. Mix.
3. Lightly coat each piece of fish with mayonnaise. Top coated fish with the seasoned breadcrumb mixture.
4. Place coated fish on prepared baking rack. Bake for 15 minutes. Heat fish to an internal temperature of 145° F or higher or until flesh is opaque and separates easily with a fork.

Yield: 6 servings, 1 fillet each
Meal Component: Meat/Meat Alternate

Herb Bagel Bites
2 whole wheat bagels, at least 3 ounces each
2 tablespoons margarine (trans fat-free)
½ teaspoons garlic powder
1 teaspoon dried basil or 2 teaspoons fresh, chopped basil

1. Preheat oven to 400° F.
2. Cut each bagel in half (if not already presliced). Then cut each half into 3 pieces.
3. Place margarine in a microwave safe bowl. Melt in the microwave for 10 seconds at a time until completely melted.
4. Add garlic powder and basil to melted margarine. Stir.
5. Place bagel pieces in a medium bowl and toss with seasoned margarine. Place on ungreased baking sheet and toast, about 7–8 minutes.

Yield: 6 servings, 2 bagel pieces each
Meal Component: Grain

Menu of the Month

Breakfast
Milk
Oatmeal (WG)
Strawberries

Morning Snack
Water
Whole Grain Pretzels
Hummus

Lunch
Milk
Baked Tilapia*
Quinoa (WG)
Green Beans
Peaches

Afternoon Snack
Water
Herb Bagel Bites* (WG)
Cherry Tomatoes

*Indicates recipes of the month.
(WG) Indicates whole grain
Baked Tilapia recipe is adapted from the Institute of Childhood Nutrition.
Herb Bagel Bites recipe is adapted from the Institute of Childhood Nutrition.

Nutrition and Fitness Notes

Provide children with a variety of nutritious, appetizing food choices. Meals that allow children to select the food and serve themselves may encourage them to try new foods and take responsibility for their food choices.

The Experienced Provider

Do not use real food as a loose part or art supply. Food items such as dry beans, peas, lentils, pasta, or rice are not loose parts and are not appropriate to add into an environment. It may seem innocent to use such food for sensory or dramatic play, but many families are facing food insecurity and food used for play could be a meal. Additionally, we do not want to send children a message that playing with food is okay.

Activities for Children

Food in Books
Share a fun book that portrays a way of life from another geographic region and pair it with a snack. An example of this is *Baby Goes to Market* by Atinuke. In this story, a baby goes to an open-air market with their mother. While there they get a bit of food from several merchants without their mother knowing. Then try some of the foods mentioned in the book, such as bananas, corn, and coconut, keeping allergies and currently introduced foods in mind.

Going to the Restaurant
Show short video clips of restaurants from varied cultures and the food they serve. Point out the differences and similarities in the menus. Show sample restaurant menus and photographs of menus and sandwich boards. Provide supplies for children to create menus, menu boards, and sandwich boards.

Culture, Community, and Food
Become familiar with the families of children in your care and in the community. Food choices, preparation methods, and eating habits are often influenced by culture and religious beliefs. Encourage and model respect for food choices.

Literacy Corner

Dim Sum for Everyone! By Grace Lin
At a restaurant, a young girl and her family enjoy dim sum, with each member of the family choosing their favorites from a teacart.

Fry Bread: A Native American Family Story by Kevin Noble Maillard
The post-colonial dish fry bread is enjoyed by modern-day Native families across many different tribes in this book that celebrates unity and togetherness through food.

Serving sizes are for ages 3–5. Guidelines for the proper credit of food may vary in some states. Please check with the CACFP in your state for more information.

JULY ATTENDANCE AND PAYMENT LOG

To record drop-off and pickup times that vary, try using two lines per child.

CHILD'S NAME	S 1	M 2	T 3	W 4	T 5	F 6	S	TOTAL	S 7	M 8	T 9	W 10	T 11	F 12	S 13	TOTAL	S 14	M 15	T 16	W 17	T 18	F 19	S 20	TOTAL	S 21	M 22	T 23	W 24	T 25	F 26	S 27	TOTAL	S 28	M 29	T 30	W 31	T	F	S	TOTAL	S	M	

JULY ATTENDANCE AND PAYMENT LOG CONTINUED

CHILD'S NAME	S	M 1	T 2	W 3	T 4	F 5	S 6	TOTAL	S 7	M 8	T 9	W 10	T 11	F 12	S 13	TOTAL	S 14	M 15	T 16	W 17	T 18	F 19	S 20	TOTAL	S 21	M 22	T 23	W 24	T 25	F 26	S 27	TOTAL	S 28	M 29	T 30	W 31	T	F	S	TOTAL	S	M

WEEKLY PAYMENT TOTALS

	FOOD PROGRAM INCOME RECVD	PARENT FEE INCOME RECVD	OTHER INCOME RECVD			
JULY INCOME				=	JUL TOTAL	
BALANCE FORWARD				=	BALANCE FWD TOTAL	
TOTAL Y-T-D INCOME				=	TOTAL Y-T-D	

Food Program Claim

Date Claim Sent _____

Date Check Received _____

MEAL COUNT TALLY

BREAKFASTS	
LUNCHES	
DINNERS	
SNACKS	

Put totals in year-end meal tally, page 95.

JULY EXPENSE REPORT

DATE	PAYMENT TYPE (cash, check #, cc #, debit)	PURCHASED FROM	PURCHASE TOTAL	ADVERTISING	INSURANCE	INTEREST	LEGAL & PROFESSIONAL SERVICES	OFFICE EXPENSES (including internet & 2nd phone)	RENT OF BUSINESS PROPERTY	REPAIR & MAINTENANCE	SUPPLIES		MILES
		THIS MONTH'S TOTAL											
		BALANCE CARRIED FORWARD											
		YEAR-TO-DATE TOTAL											

JULY EXPENSE REPORT

DATE	PAYMENT TYPE cash, check #, cc #, debit	PURCHASED FROM	PURCHASE TOTAL	TAXES & LICENSES	TRAVEL & ENTERTAINMENT	FOOD	TOYS	HOUSEHOLD ITEMS	CLEANING SUPPLIES	ACTIVITY EXPENSES			MILES
			THIS MONTH'S TOTAL										
			BALANCE CARRIED FORWARD										
			YEAR-TO-DATE TOTAL										

See page 85 for an explanation of how to transfer expenses to your tax forms.
You may wish to relabel the columns to fit your business needs.

See page 6 for an explanation of the order in which we present the categories.

AUGUST 2024

* "No. Hours Open" refers to hours from when the first child arrived to when the last child left (not your advertised work hours).
** "Other Hours Worked" refers to hours spent on business activities in the home (cleaning, meal preparation, activity planning, and so on) when children are not present.

Hours Worked
- Previous Total
- No. Hours Open*
- Other Hours Worked**
- Year-to-Date Total

SUN	MON	TUE	WED	THU	FRI	SAT
July 2024 / September 2024				1	2	3
4	5 Fire Drill Day	6	7	8	9	10
11	12	13 Tishah B'Av (Jewish)	14 Severe Storm Drill Day	15	16	17
18	19	20	21	22	23	24
25	26 Women's Equality Day	27	28	29	30 Call your local R & R agency; update your service	31

AUGUST

Art Explosions
With hands and eyes we explore art,
With all our senses—and our heart!

Recipes

Breakfast Burrito

6 eggs
1 tablespoon butter
2 cups canned black beans, rinsed and drained
3 8-inch whole wheat tortillas (at least 1 ounce each)
⅜ cup shredded mozzarella cheese
1 cup salsa

1. In a bowl, whisk eggs.
2. Heat butter in a large skillet over medium heat. When butter foams, add eggs and cook until firm, about 5 minutes.
3. When eggs are done, turn heat to low and stir in the black beans. Heat through, stirring occasionally, about 5 minutes.
4. Lay tortillas on work surface. Sprinkle each with 2 tablespoons of cheese. Place ⅔ cup of the eggs and ⅓ cup of salsa down the middle of each tortilla. Roll tortillas and cut in half.

Yield: 6 servings, ½ burrito each
Meal Component: Grain, Vegetable

Fruity Toast Snacks

3 slices whole grain bread, at least 1 ounce each
¾ cups cottage cheese
3 cups (1 cup each) sliced kiwi, strawberries, and bananas

1. Toast bread. Spread ¼ cup cottage cheese on each slice.
2. Top with ¼ cup fruit slices. Cut in half. Serve remaining ¼ cup fruit on the side.

Yield: 6 servings, ½ slice plus ¼ cup fruit on the side
Meal Component: Grain, Fruit

Serving sizes are for ages 3–5. Guidelines for the proper credit of food may vary in some states. Please check with the CACFP in your state for more information.

Menu of the Month

Breakfast
Milk
Breakfast Burrito* (WG)

Morning Snack
Water
Fruity Toast Snacks* (WG)

Lunch
Milk
Whole Wheat Spaghetti (WG)
Turkey Meatballs
Zucchini Spears
Pitted Cherries

Afternoon Snack
Water
Cantaloupe Slices
Yogurt

*Indicates recipes of the month.
(WG) Indicates whole grain
Breakfast Burrito recipe is adapted from page 51 of *Look & Cook for Family Child Care Homes*.
Fruity Toast Snacks recipe is adapted from page 176 of *Look & Cook for Family Child Care Homes*.

Nutrition and Fitness Notes

Children explore food with all their senses. Fresh produce provides a rainbow of colors: red strawberries, green broccoli, and yellow squash. The smell of a grilling hamburger or baking cookies may entice children. Children hear the sounds produced by the food and explore texture and temperature. Finally, children taste the food and discover whether it is sweet, sour, salty, or spicy.

The Experienced Provider

Some children are drawn to messy activities that others approach hesitantly or not at all. Some children may find certain sensory stimuli to be calming while others find it to be stressful. For example, some children may cover their hands in paint, others will use paintbrushes, and others will worry about getting near the paint. Allowing children to find this out on their own as part of play fosters their self-regulation.

Activities for Children

Skin Tone Paint
Put a sensory spin on skin tone paint mixing activities. Let children choose human skin tone paints to put into sealable plastic bags. Then portion the paint into the bags, seal them up, and allow children to squeeze and mix the paint inside of the bags. Children can use their new paint colors for painting human cutouts that are then displayed in the room to represent the diversity of skin tones.

Floorbooks
Floorbooks are large-scale blank books that children add to throughout the day. The content of these books is up to the children, and often they choose to make marks and drawings about their play, explorations, or trips outside of the school. The adult may act as a scribe if the child is not comfortable or ready to begin mark-making or forming words in print but should not take over the content. This content—and what is not present—tells us a lot about how children are experiencing and interpreting their experiences in the world.

Celebrating Dark Skin Tones
Prevailing messages about the negativity of darkness in general intersect with our ideas about skin color. Educators can celebrate dark skin tones in various ways, by (1) celebrating all skin tones, (2) focusing on darker hues specifically, (3) discussing why we have differences in skin tones, and (4) celebrating people with dark skin tones.

Literacy Corner

Noisy Paint Box by Barb Rosenstock
Young Vasya Kandinsky, one of the first abstract painters, had a unique connection to colors, experiencing colors as sounds and sounds as colors. Refusing to paint the way everyone expected him to, Kandinsky trusted his instincts and made something new and beautiful.

Maybe Something Beautiful by Isabel Campoy and Theresa Howell
A gray city neighborhood is transformed when a young artist partners with a muralist to bring the drab walls to life. This story is based on the true story of the Urban Art Trail in San Diego.

AUGUST ATTENDANCE AND PAYMENT LOG

To record drop-off and pickup times that vary, try using two lines per child.

CHILD'S NAME	S	M	T	W	T	F	S	TOTAL	S	M	T	W	T	F	S	TOTAL	S	M	T	W	T	F	S	TOTAL	S	M	T	W	T	F	S	TOTAL	S	M
	1	2	3						4	5	6	7	8	9	10		11	12	13	14	15	16	17		18	19	20	21	22	23	24		25	26	27	28	29	30	31			

AUGUST ATTENDANCE AND PAYMENT LOG CONTINUED

CHILD'S NAME	S	M	T 1	W 2	T	F	S 3	TOTAL	S 4	M 5	T 6	W 7	T 8	F 9	S 10	TOTAL	S 11	M 12	T 13	W 14	T 15	F 16	S 17	TOTAL	S 18	M 19	T 20	W 21	T 22	F 23	S 24	TOTAL	S 25	M 26	T 27	W 28	T 29	F 30	S 31	TOTAL	S	M

WEEKLY PAYMENT TOTALS

	FOOD PROGRAM INCOME RECVD	PARENT FEE INCOME RECVD	OTHER INCOME RECVD		
AUGUST INCOME				=	AUG TOTAL
BALANCE FORWARD				=	BALANCE FWD TOTAL
TOTAL Y-T-D INCOME				=	TOTAL Y-T-D

Food Program Claim

Date Claim Sent _____

Date Check Received _____

MEAL COUNT TALLY

BREAKFASTS	
LUNCHES	
DINNERS	
SNACKS	

Put totals in year-end meal tally, page 95.

AUGUST EXPENSE REPORT

DATE	PAYMENT TYPE cash, check #, cc #, debit	PURCHASED FROM	PURCHASE TOTAL	ADVERTISING	INSURANCE	INTEREST	LEGAL & PROFESSIONAL SERVICES	OFFICE EXPENSES (including internet & 2nd phone)	RENT OF BUSINESS PROPERTY	REPAIR & MAINTENANCE	SUPPLIES		MILES
		THIS MONTH'S TOTAL											
		BALANCE CARRIED FORWARD											
		YEAR-TO-DATE TOTAL											

AUGUST EXPENSE REPORT

DATE	PAYMENT TYPE cash, check #, cc #, debit	PURCHASED FROM	PURCHASE TOTAL	TAXES & LICENSES	TRAVEL & ENTERTAINMENT	FOOD	TOYS	HOUSEHOLD ITEMS	CLEANING SUPPLIES	ACTIVITY EXPENSES			MILES
		THIS MONTH'S TOTAL											
		BALANCE CARRIED FORWARD											
		YEAR-TO-DATE TOTAL											

See page 85 for an explanation of how to transfer expenses to your tax forms.
You may wish to relabel the columns to fit your business needs.

See page 6 for an explanation of the order in which we present the categories.

SEPTEMBER 2024

Hours Worked	
Previous Total	
No. Hours Open*	
Other Hours Worked**	
Year-to-Date Total	

* "No. Hours Open" refers to hours from when the first child arrived to when the last child left (not your advertised work hours).
** "Other Hours Worked" refers to hours spent on business activities in the home (cleaning, meal preparation, activity planning, and so on) when children are not present.

SUN	MON	TUE	WED	THU	FRI	SAT
1	**2** Labor Day	**3** Fire Drill Day	**4**	**5**	**6**	**7**
8 Grandparents' Day	**9**	**10**	**11** Patriot Day; Severe Storm Drill Day	**12**	**13**	**14**
15 Start of National Hispanic Heritage Month	**16** Mawlid al-Nabi (Islamic); 2024 3rd quarter estimated taxes due	**17** Constitution Day	**18**	**19**	**20**	**21**
22 Autumn begins; Change your smoke alarm and carbon monoxide filter batteries	**23**	**24**	**25**	**26**	**27** Native Americans Day	**28**
29	**30** Call your local R & R agency; update your service					

The Redleaf Calendar-Keeper™ 2025 is available now!

AUGUST 2024

S	M	T	W	T	F	S
				1	2	3
4	5	6	7	8	9	10
11	12	13	14	15	16	17
18	19	20	21	22	23	24
25	26	27	28	29	30	31

OCTOBER 2024

S	M	T	W	T	F	S
		1	2	3	4	5
6	7	8	9	10	11	12
13	14	15	16	17	18	19
20	21	22	23	24	25	26
27	28	29	30	31		

SEPTEMBER

We Are Scientists
Science is a state of mind,
Ask your questions, then seek to find!

Recipes

Nut Butter Pita Pockets
3 whole wheat pita rounds, at least 1 ounce each
6 tablespoons peanut butter
1½ cup thinly sliced apple
1½ cup thinly sliced pear

1. Cut each pita round in half. Spread 1 tablespoon of peanut butter in each pita pocket half.
2. Put 2 apple and 2 pear slices in each pita half. Serve the rest of the apples and pears on the side.

Yield: 6 servings, ½-pita sandwiches plus additional apple and pear slices
Meal Component: Grain, Meat/Meat Alternate, Fruit

Pizza Sandwich
2 tablespoons butter
3 cups diced zucchini
¾ cup marinara sauce
3 whole wheat hoagie buns, at least 1 ounce each
2¼ cups shredded mozzarella cheese

1. Preheat oven to 400° F. Line a baking sheet with foil.
2. Melt butter in a large skillet over medium heat. Add zucchini and sauté until tender, about 5 minutes.
3. Add marinara sauce and cook until sauce is heated, about 2 minutes.
4. Slice open hoagie buns, keeping a hinge. Open and lay flat on the baking sheet. Fill each bun with ⅓ of the zucchini sauce and top with a heaping ¾ cup of mozzarella cheese.
5. Heat sandwiches in oven until cheese melts, about 3 minutes. Cut in half to serve.

Yield: 6 servings, ½ sandwich each
Meal Component: Grain, Meat/Meat Alternate, Vegetable

Serving sizes are for ages 3–5. Guidelines for the proper credit of food may vary in some states. Please check with the CACFP in your state for more information.

Menu of the Month

Breakfast
Milk
Nut Butter Pita Pockets* (WG)

Morning Snack
Water
Kohlrabi Chunks
Plain Popcorn (WG)

Lunch
Milk
Pizza Sandwich* (WG)
Watermelon Chunks

Afternoon Snack
Water
Raspberries
Walnuts

*Indicates recipes of the month.
(WG) Indicates whole grain
Nut Butter Pita Pockets recipe is adapted from the Institute of Childhood Nutrition.
Pizza Sandwich recipe is adapted from page 83 of *Look & Cook for Family Child Care Homes*.

Nutrition and Fitness Notes

Young children may not fully understand how to categorize foods into specific food groups, such as fruits, vegetables, grains, and dairy. Instead, children may enjoy sorting foods by characteristics such as color, texture, and preparation method.

The Experienced Provider

One of educators' most important roles is creating play opportunities that challenge children to solve problems. Ask critical-thinking questions such as: How else can we investigate this? How many ways can you group the bottle caps? How do you know that the blocks worked? What else can you use? How would other children respond to your idea? How can you include them?

Activities for Children

Texture Scavenger Hunt
Create a scavenger hunt sheet with words and pictures of different textures children will look for. Some possibilities for textures include *smooth*, *rough*, *bumpy*, *soft*, and *hard*. Each child needs a scavenger hunt sheet and a writing utensil to mark off the textures they find. Then children use their sense of touch to search for the textures indoors and outside. They can report their findings once the hunt has ended.

Teaching with Tech
Young children must be exposed to a variety of technologies and explicitly taught how to use those technology tools in a safe and responsible manner. Some ideas: Show weather applications on a tablet when discussing the weather. Use digital timers for games. Make audio recordings of yourself or children counting to one hundred and videos of objects being counted. Provide tablet-based digital observation logs for children to note what they observe in science experiments and digital cameras or tablets for taking photographs.

Acknowledging Differences
Acknowledging differences allows the children and adults to appreciate both differences and similarities. Pretending to not notice that a child uses a wheelchair means you are not noticing that child, whereas acknowledging the wheelchair but not making assumptions about what the child can and cannot do honors the child.

Literacy Corner

On a Beam of Light by Jennifer Berne
Albert Einstein was once a curious, inquisitive child who asked all the questions, even questions no one had thought to ask before. As he grew, he never stopped looking hard for answers.

Up, Down, and Around by Katherine Ayres
An abundance of vegetables growing up, down, and around the garden shares the magic of growing plants with children.

SEPTEMBER ATTENDANCE AND PAYMENT LOG

To record drop-off and pickup times that vary, try using two lines per child.

CHILD'S NAME	S 1	M 2	T 3	W 4	T 5	F 6	S 7	TOTAL	S 8	M 9	T 10	W 11	T 12	F 13	S 14	TOTAL	S 15	M 16	T 17	W 18	T 19	F 20	S 21	TOTAL	S 22	M 23	T 24	W 25	T 26	F 27	S 28	TOTAL	S 29	M 30	T	W	T	F	S	TOTAL	S	M

SEPTEMBER ATTENDANCE AND PAYMENT LOG CONTINUED

CHILD'S NAME	S 1	M 2	T 3	W 4	T 5	F 6	S 7	TOTAL	S 8	M 9	T 10	W 11	T 12	F 13	S 14	TOTAL	S 15	M 16	T 17	W 18	T 19	F 20	S 21	TOTAL	S 22	M 23	T 24	W 25	T 26	F 27	S 28	TOTAL	S 29	M 30	T	W	T	F	S	TOTAL	S	M
WEEKLY PAYMENT TOTALS																																										

	FOOD PROGRAM INCOME RECVD	PARENT FEE INCOME RECVD	OTHER INCOME RECVD			
SEPTEMBER INCOME				=	SEPT TOTAL	
BALANCE FORWARD				=	BALANCE FWD TOTAL	
TOTAL Y-T-D INCOME				=	TOTAL Y-T-D	

Food Program Claim

Date Claim Sent _____

Date Check Received _____

MEAL COUNT TALLY

BREAKFASTS	
LUNCHES	
DINNERS	
SNACKS	

Put totals in year-end meal tally, page 95.

SEPTEMBER EXPENSE REPORT

DATE	PAYMENT TYPE cash, check #, cc #, debit	PURCHASED FROM	PURCHASE TOTAL	ADVERTISING	INSURANCE	INTEREST	LEGAL & PROFESSIONAL SERVICES	OFFICE EXPENSES (including internet & 2nd phone)	RENT OF BUSINESS PROPERTY	REPAIR & MAINTENANCE	SUPPLIES		MILES
		THIS MONTH'S TOTAL											
		BALANCE CARRIED FORWARD											
		YEAR-TO-DATE TOTAL											

SEPTEMBER EXPENSE REPORT

DATE	PAYMENT TYPE cash, check #, cc #, debit	PURCHASED FROM	PURCHASE TOTAL	TAXES & LICENSES	TRAVEL & ENTERTAINMENT	FOOD	TOYS	HOUSEHOLD ITEMS	CLEANING SUPPLIES	ACTIVITY EXPENSES			MILES
		THIS MONTH'S TOTAL											
		BALANCE CARRIED FORWARD											
		YEAR-TO-DATE TOTAL											

See page 85 for an explanation of how to transfer expenses to your tax forms. You may wish to relabel the columns to fit your business needs.

See page 6 for an explanation of the order in which we present the categories.

OCTOBER 2024

* "No. Hours Open" refers to hours from when the first child arrived to when the last child left (not your advertised work hours).
** "Other Hours Worked" refers to hours spent on business activities in the home (cleaning, meal preparation, activity planning, and so on) when children are not present.

Hours Worked
Previous Total
No. Hours Open*
Other Hours Worked**
Year-to-Date Total

SUN	MON	TUE	WED	THU	FRI	SAT
		1 National Bullying Prevention Month Breast Cancer Awareness Month	2	3 Rosh Hashanah (Jewish)	4	5
6	7 Child Health Day Fire Drill Day	8	9 Severe Storm Drill Day	10	11	12 Yom Kippur (Jewish)
13	14 Columbus Day Indigenous Peoples Day	15 End of National Hispanic Heritage Month	16	17 Sukkot begins (Jewish)	18	19
20	21	22	23 Sukkot ends (Jewish)	24	25	26
27	28	29	30 Call your local R & R agency; update your service	31 Halloween Diwali (Hindu)		

SEPTEMBER 2024

S	M	T	W	T	F	S
1	2	3	4	5	6	7
8	9	10	11	12	13	14
15	16	17	18	19	20	21
22	23	24	25	26	27	28
29	30					

NOVEMBER 2024

S	M	T	W	T	F	S
					1	2
3	4	5	6	7	8	9
10	11	12	13	14	15	16
17	18	19	20	21	22	23
24	25	26	27	28	29	30

Time Flies
When You're Running a Business!

Now is the perfect time to place your order for the business essentials you'll need next year. Order now and you'll be ready to go for 2025.

The Redleaf Calendar-Keeper™ 2025
A Record-Keeping System for Family Child Care Professionals

Year after year, the *Redleaf Press Calendar-Keeper* is the most reliable organizational resource for family child care professionals. Continue to save time and money by ordering your 2025 edition now!

#100025-CK24 $21.95

Family Child Care Business Receipt Book

Improve your record keeping with receipts designed specifically for family child care. Three books, each with 50 carbonless duplicate sets of receipts, are included.

#106101-CK24 $15.95

Family Child Care Mileage-Keeper

Record business trips, repairs, tolls, parking, and other car expenses. Forms are included for one year's worth of records.

#104101-CK24 $7.95

Family Child Care Inventory-Keeper

Track furniture, appliances, and other property used in your business for depreciation and insurance purposes.

#107001-CK24 $14.95

Family Child Care Sharing in the Caring
Agreement Packet for Parents and Providers

Establish a clear understanding with parents from the start. This packet contains five copies of a formal two-part agreement form as well as instructions for how to complete contract terms for rates, holidays, vacations, payment dates, and illnesses.

#101301-CK24 $9.95
Forms only (pack of five) #101601-CK24 $8.95

See pages 5 and 66 for additional resources.

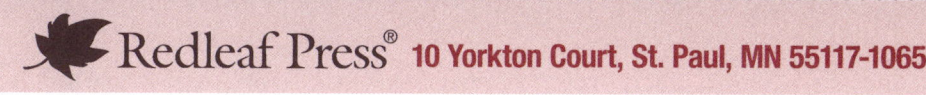

Redleaf Press® 10 Yorkton Court, St. Paul, MN 55117-1065

Call 800-423-8309 • Fax 800-641-0115 • www.redleafpress.org

Name _____

Address _____ Apt. ____

City _____

State [ ]   Zip Code [   ]-[   ]   **24CK**

Daytime phone (____) _____ E-mail _____

QTY	ITEM #	TITLE	CATALOG PRICE	AMOUNT

Shipping & Handling Charges

Order Size..........Add
$0 to $49.99.........$7.95
$50.00 to $99.99.....$10.95
$100.00 to $149.99...$13.95
$150.00 or more......10% of net order

SUBTOTAL [ ]
Shipping/Handling [ ]
Your applicable state* and county sales TAX [ ]
TOTAL [ ]

Alaska, Hawaii, and APO orders are shipped by priority mail; standard rates apply. Foreign orders are shipped by U.S. Postal Service. Call for pricing.

*We currently collect sales tax in these states: IL, IN, MD, MI, MN, NC, OK, PA, TN, VA, WA, WI.

Payment: (U.S. funds only. Sorry, we cannot accept COD orders.)

[ ] Check or money order enclosed. DO NOT send cash.

Charge to credit card: [ ] Visa [ ] MC [ ] Discover [ ] American Express

Expiration Date [ ][ ] Month Year

[   ] CVN (3-digit code on the back of card)

Cardholder signature (required) _____

Prices subject to change without notice.

Tom Copeland Resources

Tom Copeland, JD, is a licensed attorney, leading tax specialist, and award-winning advocate for the business of family child care.

NEW! Family Child Care 2023 Tax Workbook and Organizer

Tom Copeland is the nation's leading expert on the business of family child care. Updated annually, this is the most comprehensive resource available. This edition contains guidance on navigating new tax laws, tips to help save money, and tools that take the guesswork out of family child care business taxes. Softbound, 264 pgs.

#100823-CK24 $21.95

NEW! Family Child Care 2023 Tax Companion

The *Tax Companion* is a comprehensive tool that will help tax preparers understand the rules that affect family child care businesses. It also includes information on the new tax laws that relate to depreciation. Using this resource will increase your confidence in the tax professionals who prepare your return, help you identify potential errors before your taxes are filed, and ensure that your tax preparer is claiming all allowable deductions. Softbound, 80 pgs.

#101023-CK24 $21.95

The Business of Family Child Care: Contacts and Policies

Most family child care providers would rather care for children than write and enforce contracts and policies, but taking care of the children is only part of the job. Contracts and policies are another important part of running a business. This video can help you understand how to establish a good business relationship with the families you serve by creating clear contracts and policies and enforcing them fairly.

#548029-CK24 $49.95

The Business of Family Child Care: Record-Keeping

Most family child care providers would rather care for children than spend time keeping records. But record keeping is an important part of running a business. This training video can help you understand proper record-keeping strategies, help lower taxes, and save family child care providers money.

#547329-CK24 $79.95

Family Child Care Record-Keeping Guide, 9th Edition

Keep your business organized with the latest information and advice to help you maintain important records. This edition includes descriptions of new depreciation rules, clarifications on deductions, updated resource links, and much more. Softbound, 216 pgs.

#543970-CK24 $21.95

Family Child Care Contracts and Policies, 4th Edition

This edition of the family child care classic offers expanded information on handling rates, late payments, and other fees in your contract; resolving disputes with clients; writing comprehensive policies; and enforcing and terminating your contract. Softbound, 184 pgs.

#546506-CK24 $21.95

Family Child Care Marketing Guide, 2nd Edition

Maximize your enrollment and find inexpensive ways to promote your business. Dozens of marketing tips, information on setting rates, and guidance for using electronic media are included. Softbound, 216 pgs.

#541129-CK24 $18.95

Family Child Care Legal and Insurance Guide

From purchasing insurance to incorporating your business, this indispensable guide details the ways you can reduce the risks and ensure the health and prosperity of your business. Softbound, 224 pgs.

#108501-CK24 $21.95

Family Child Care Business Planning Guide

Whether you're just starting out or have an established operation, a business plan is an essential tool for success. Find information on how to write and use your plan to effectively manage your business. Softbound, 96 pgs.

#112901-CK24 $21.95

Family Child Care Money Management and Retirement Guide

Find valuable information for your business, including how to earn more money and reduce your expenses, plan for retirement, and handle special financial situations. Softbound, 208 pgs.

#112801-CK24 $18.95

OCTOBER

Learning Self-Regulation
Sometimes I get sad or stressed,
My mind and body need a rest!

Recipes

Oatmeal Chocolate Chip Breakfast Treats

2 medium ripe bananas
1¼ cups quick-cooking oats
¼ cup mini chocolate chips

1. Preheat oven to 375° F. Coat a baking sheet with cooking spray.
2. In a bowl, mash the bananas. Add the oats and chocolate chips and combine well.
3. Drop one heaping tablespoon of batter on the baking sheet for each treat. There should be 18.
4. Bake for 15 minutes.

Yield: 6 servings, 3 treats each
Meal Component: Grain

Cheesy Bean Tostada

¾ cup fat-free, low-sodium refried beans
6 corn tortillas, at least ½ ounce each
6 tablespoons shredded cheddar cheese

1. Preheat oven to 400° F.
2. Spread 2 tablespoons of beans on each corn tortilla.
3. Sprinkle 1 tablespoon of cheese evenly over the beans on each tortilla.
4. Place on ungreased baking sheet and bake for 7 minutes or until cheese is melted.

Yield: 6 servings, 1 tostada each
Meal Component: Meat/Meat Alternate, Grain

Serving sizes are for ages 3–5. Guidelines for the proper credit of food may vary in some states. Please check with the CACFP in your state for more information.

Menu of the Month

Breakfast
Milk
Oatmeal Chocolate Chip Breakfast Treats* (WG)
Blackberries

Morning Snack
Water
Cheesy Bean Tostada* (WG)

Lunch
Milk
Grilled Ham and Cheese Sandwiches
Frozen Vegetable Medley
Pear Slices

Afternoon Snack
100% Apple Juice
Cottage Cheese

*Indicates recipes of the month.
(WG) Indicates whole grain
Oatmeal Chocolate Chip Breakfast Treats recipe is adapted from page 43 of *Look & Cook for Family Child Care Homes*.
Cheesy Bean Tostada recipe is adapted from the Institute of Childhood Nutrition.

Nutrition and Fitness Notes

Children must have water available to them throughout the day. They can become dehydrated very quickly. As children learn their hunger cues, they also begin to recognize when they are thirsty. Thirst is an important concept; many people (including adults) mistake thirst for hunger, resulting in unnecessary overeating.

The Experienced Provider

Often when we feel stressed about a child's behavior we say they are "looking for attention." If we adjust our framing to say this child is "looking for connection," we can view this same behavior in a new light. Children who are struggling are often seeking connection using the tools they have. We can help children in these situations by intentionally connecting more with them and focusing on their strengths.

Activities for Children

Rest Time
Most young children need to rest or relax at some time during the day. Without adult guidance to rest, children may become exhausted, overstimulated, or stressed without being aware of how they are feeling. Establish a routine when preparing for rest time. Encourage children to help with placing cots and getting their sheets or blankets from their individual storage spaces. Lowering the lights and playing soft music can create a soothing environment. Read, sing quietly, or provide other relaxation activities leading into and during rest time.

Cleanup Transitions
Cleaning up often signals a transition, leaving the familiar experience to move into the new one. Saying "reset the learning environment" over "clean up" or "pack up" communicates that there will be an opportunity to return to the experience. Music can initiate transitions. Sing as children reset their materials or play music while they dance to a meeting area. There is no need to say, "We're waiting for you," or "Show me you're ready," because everyone participates in the shared ritual of singing and moving.

Neurodivergence
All young children get overwhelmed by sensory stimuli at times, but neurodivergent children tend to do this more often. This is a combination of the way neurodivergent children process sensory information and the environments they find themselves in. While we cannot control how a child processes sensory information, we can make our programs more sensory aware.

Literacy Corner

When You Just Have to Roar! by Rachel Robertson
Ms. Mya's class is having a chaotic day until the teacher steps in to set expectations and helpfully guide the children toward positive behaviors that improve everyone's experience.

It's Hard to be Five: Learning How to Work My Control Panel by Jamie Lee Curtis
Being five and practicing self-control is a tough combination, but Curtis brings some fun to the struggle with her cheerful, silly text matched with playful illustrations.

OCTOBER ATTENDANCE AND PAYMENT LOG

To record drop-off and pickup times that vary, try using two lines per child.

CHILD'S NAME	S	M	T	W	T	F	S	TOTAL	S	M	T	W	T	F	S	TOTAL	S	M	T	W	T	F	S	TOTAL	S	M	T	W	T	F	S	TOTAL	S	M
	1	2	3	4	5				6	7	8	9	10	11	12		13	14	15	16	17	18	19		20	21	22	23	24	25	26		27	28	29	30	31		

OCTOBER ATTENDANCE AND PAYMENT LOG CONTINUED

CHILD'S NAME	S	M 1	T 2	W 3	T 4	F 5	S	TOTAL	S 6	M 7	T 8	W 9	T 10	F 11	S 12	TOTAL	S 13	M 14	T 15	W 16	T 17	F 18	S 19	TOTAL	S 20	M 21	T 22	W 23	T 24	F 25	S 26	TOTAL	S 27	M 28	T 29	W 30	T 31	F	S	TOTAL	S	M
WEEKLY PAYMENT TOTALS																																											

	FOOD PROGRAM INCOME RECVD	PARENT FEE INCOME RECVD	OTHER INCOME RECVD			
OCTOBER INCOME				=	OCT TOTAL	
BALANCE FORWARD				=	BALANCE FWD TOTAL	
TOTAL Y-T-D INCOME				=	TOTAL Y-T-D	

Food Program Claim

Date Claim Sent _____

Date Check Received _____

MEAL COUNT TALLY

BREAKFASTS	
LUNCHES	
DINNERS	
SNACKS	

Put totals in year-end meal tally, page 95.

OCTOBER EXPENSE REPORT

DATE	PAYMENT TYPE cash, check #, cc #, debit	PURCHASED FROM	PURCHASE TOTAL	ADVERTISING	INSURANCE	INTEREST	LEGAL & PROFESSIONAL SERVICES	OFFICE EXPENSES (including internet & 2nd phone)	RENT OF BUSINESS PROPERTY	REPAIR & MAINTENANCE	SUPPLIES		MILES
		THIS MONTH'S TOTAL											
		BALANCE CARRIED FORWARD											
		YEAR-TO-DATE TOTAL											

OCTOBER EXPENSE REPORT

DATE	PAYMENT TYPE cash, check #, cc #, debit	PURCHASED FROM	PURCHASE TOTAL	TAXES & LICENSES	TRAVEL & ENTERTAINMENT	FOOD	TOYS	HOUSEHOLD ITEMS	CLEANING SUPPLIES	ACTIVITY EXPENSES			MILES
		THIS MONTH'S TOTAL											
		BALANCE CARRIED FORWARD											
		YEAR-TO-DATE TOTAL											

See page 85 for an explanation of how to transfer expenses to your tax forms.
You may wish to relabel the columns to fit your business needs.

See page 6 for an explanation of the order in which we present the categories.

NOVEMBER 2024

Hours Worked
- Previous Total
- No. Hours Open*
- Other Hours Worked**
- Year-to-Date Total

* "No. Hours Open" refers to hours from when the first child arrived to when the last child left (not your advertised work hours).
** "Other Hours Worked" refers to hours spent on business activities in the home (cleaning, meal preparation, activity planning, and so on) when children are not present.

Be ready for 2025. Order your Redleaf Calendar-Keeper™ 2025 today.

SUN	MON	TUE	WED	THU	FRI	SAT
					1 American Indian Heritage Month; All Saints' Day (Catholic)	**2** Día de los Muertos; All Souls' Day (Catholic)
3	**4** Fire Drill Day	**5** Election Day	**6**	**7**	**8**	**9**
10	**11** Veterans Day	**12**	**13** Severe Storm Drill Day	**14**	**15**	**16**
17	**18**	**19**	**20** Universal Children's Day	**21**	**22**	**23**
24	**25**	**26**	**27** Call your local R & R agency; update your service	**28** Thanksgiving Day	**29**	**30**

OCTOBER 2024
S	M	T	W	T	F	S
		1	2	3	4	5
6	7	8	9	10	11	12
13	14	15	16	17	18	19
20	21	22	23	24	25	26
27	28	29	30	31		

DECEMBER 2024
S	M	T	W	T	F	S
1	2	3	4	5	6	7
8	9	10	11	12	13	14
15	16	17	18	19	20	21
22	23	24	25	26	27	28
29	30	31				

NOVEMBER

Just Dance
Move your body to the beat,
Wave your arms and tap your feet!

Recipes

Overnight Oats and Berries

¼ cup 1% milk
¾ cup vanilla nonfat Greek yogurt
2 teaspoons pasteurized honey
¼ teaspoon vanilla extract
1 cup quick oats
3 cups mixed frozen berries (unsweetened)
1½ cups fresh berries or sliced fruit

1. In a medium bowl, combine milk, Greek yogurt, honey, and vanilla extract. Stir.
2. Add oats. Mix well. Then add berries and stir again.
3. Cover and refrigerate for 8–12 hours.
4. When ready to serve, remove from the refrigerator, stir, and divide into 6 bowls. Top each serving with ¼ cup fresh fruit.

Yield: 6 servings, ¾ cup each
Meal Component: Grain, fruit

Shredded Beef Sandwich

½ cup ketchup
1 tablespoon Worcestershire sauce
1 tablespoon Dijon mustard
¼ teaspoon garlic powder
1 pound boneless chuck roast
3 whole wheat hamburger buns, at least 1 ounce each

1. Preheat oven to 350° F. Line a small baking pan with foil.
2. In a small bowl, mix ketchup, Worcestershire sauce, mustard, and garlic powder. Brush or rub on all sides of the roast.
3. Place roast in baking pan and bake uncovered until very tender, about 2 hours. Remove from oven, cut into quarters, and allow to cool for about 15 minutes.
4. Shred meat with two forks and mix in the pan juices.
5. Fill each bun with 3 ounces of shredded beef. Cut in half.

Yield: 6 servings, ½ sandwich each
Meal Component: Grain, Meat/Meat Alternate

Menu of the Month

Breakfast
Milk
Overnight Oats and Berries* (WG)

Morning Snack
Water
Mixed Apple Chunks and Pomegranate Seeds
Pistachios

Lunch
Milk
Shredded Beef Sandwich* (WG)
Steamed Carrots
Mandarin Oranges

Afternoon Snack
Bean Dip
Mixed Fresh Vegetables

*Indicates recipes of the month.
(WG) Indicates whole grain
Overnight Oats and Berries recipe is adapted from the Institute of Childhood Nutrition.
Shredded Beef Sandwich recipe is adapted from page 86 of *Look & Cook for Family Child Care Homes*.

Nutrition and Fitness Notes

Active play is essential to optimal physical development, fitness, and the overall health of young children. The benefits of active physical play throughout the day are many: increased physical development and fitness, improved weight management, increased self-esteem, and enhanced learning readiness, among many others.

The Experienced Provider

Encourage all children to try a variety of activities and to develop skill and enjoyment in moving their bodies. Promote movement, activity, and fun—not competitiveness. Encourage families to participate in physical activities with their children, and remind them that physical skills and motor coordination do not improve just through aging; improvement requires demonstration, teaching, and practice.

Activities for Children

Dance Party
Show samples of dance or music videos to the children. Divide them into small groups, and ask each group to choose music, design costumes, choreograph a dance routine, and perform their dance for the other groups. Alternately, ask children to observe and count how many times people run, hop, skip, jump, or kick. Occasionally pause the video and ask children to try to mimic certain movements they have just viewed.

Dance Like Melanin
Make cards with different skin colors on them and a music playlist with songs of various tempos. Then read aloud a book such as *All the Colors We Are: The Story of How We Get Our Skin Color* that explains variations in skin hues by how active someone's melanin is. Tell children they will move their bodies more quickly for colors that have more active melanin and more slowly for colors that have less active melanin. Hold up a color with more active melanin and play an up-tempo song that allows the children to move quickly. Then hold up a skin color with less active melanin, and play a slow song so children move slowly. Play songs that are neither fast nor slow for mid skin tones.

Access Not Diagnosis
You don't need to know the medical diagnosis of a child who uses a wheelchair—rather, consider whether they can access all areas and materials in the classroom. Can they get in and out of the chair themselves? Are they able to play on the floor? The same principal is true for mental health and neurodivergence.

Literacy Corner

I Will Dance by Nancy Bo Flood
Dancing is for everybody. Come with Eva and her motorized wheelchair as she swirls her way from audition to performance with other dancers of all abilities.

Kitchen Dance by Maurie J. Manning
Although they are supposed to be in bed, the young narrator and her little brother find themselves swept up in the loving embrace of their parents as they tango through kitchen cleanup.

NOVEMBER ATTENDANCE AND PAYMENT LOG

To record drop-off and pickup times that vary, try using two lines per child.

CHILD'S NAME	S	M	T	W	T	F 1	S 2	TOTAL	S 3	M 4	T 5	W 6	T 7	F 8	S 9	TOTAL	S 10	M 11	T 12	W 13	T 14	F 15	S 16	TOTAL	S 17	M 18	T 19	W 20	T 21	F 22	S 23	TOTAL	S 24	M 25	T 26	W 27	T 28	F 29	S 30	TOTAL	S	M

NOVEMBER ATTENDANCE AND PAYMENT LOG CONTINUED

CHILD'S NAME	S	M	T	W	T	F	S	TOTAL	S	M	T	W	T	F	S	TOTAL	S	M	T	W	T	F	S	TOTAL	S	M	T	W	T	F	S	TOTAL	S	M	T	W	T	F	S	TOTAL	S	M
						1	2		3	4	5	6	7	8	9		10	11	12	13	14	15	16		17	18	19	20	21	22	23		24	25	26	27	28	29	30			

WEEKLY PAYMENT TOTALS

	FOOD PROGRAM INCOME RECVD	PARENT FEE INCOME RECVD	OTHER INCOME RECVD			
NOVEMBER INCOME				=	NOV TOTAL	
BALANCE FORWARD				=	BALANCE FWD TOTAL	
TOTAL Y-T-D INCOME				=	TOTAL Y-T-D	

Food Program Claim

Date Claim Sent _____

Date Check Received _____

MEAL COUNT TALLY

BREAKFASTS	
LUNCHES	
DINNERS	
SNACKS	

Put totals in year-end meal tally, page 95.

NOVEMBER EXPENSE REPORT

DATE	PAYMENT TYPE cash, check #, cc #, debit	PURCHASED FROM	PURCHASE TOTAL	ADVERTISING	INSURANCE	INTEREST	LEGAL & PROFESSIONAL SERVICES	OFFICE EXPENSES (including internet & 2nd phone)	RENT OF BUSINESS PROPERTY	REPAIR & MAINTENANCE	SUPPLIES		MILES
		THIS MONTH'S TOTAL											
		BALANCE CARRIED FORWARD											
		YEAR-TO-DATE TOTAL											

NOVEMBER EXPENSE REPORT

DATE	PAYMENT TYPE cash, check #, cc #, debit	PURCHASED FROM	PURCHASE TOTAL	TAXES & LICENSES	TRAVEL & ENTERTAINMENT	FOOD	TOYS	HOUSEHOLD ITEMS	CLEANING SUPPLIES	ACTIVITY EXPENSES			MILES
		THIS MONTH'S TOTAL											
		BALANCE CARRIED FORWARD											
		YEAR-TO-DATE TOTAL											

See page 85 for an explanation of how to transfer expenses to your tax forms. You may wish to relabel the columns to fit your business needs.

See page 6 for an explanation of the order in which we present the categories.

DECEMBER 2024

Hours Worked
- Previous Total
- No. Hours Open*
- Other Hours Worked**
- Year-to-Date Total

* "No. Hours Open" refers to hours from when the first child arrived to when the last child left (not your advertised work hours).

** "Other Hours Worked" refers to hours spent on business activities in the home (cleaning, meal preparation, activity planning, and so on) when children are not present.

SUN	MON	TUE	WED	THU	FRI	SAT
1 First Sunday of Advent (Christian)	**2** Fire Drill Day	**3**	**4**	**5**	**6**	**7**
8	**9**	**10** Human Rights Day	**11** Severe Storm Drill Day	**12**	**13**	**14**
15	**16**	**17**	**18**	**19**	**20**	**21** Winter begins
22	**23**	**24** Christmas Eve (Christian)	**25** Christmas Day (Christian)	**26** Hanukkah begins (Jewish) Boxing Day Kwanzaa begins	**27**	**28**
29	**30** Call your local R & R agency; update your service	**31** New Year's Eve				

Tax season is just around the corner. Don't forget to order your 2024 tax resources!

NOVEMBER 2024

S	M	T	W	T	F	S
					1	2
3	4	5	6	7	8	9
10	11	12	13	14	15	16
17	18	19	20	21	22	23
24	25	26	27	28	29	30

JANUARY 2025

S	M	T	W	T	F	S
			1	2	3	4
5	6	7	8	9	10	11
12	13	14	15	16	17	18
19	20	21	22	23	24	25
26	27	28	29	30	31	

DECEMBER

Celebrating Families
I love my family every day,
With all my heart, in every way!

Recipes

Pineapple Chicken

2 tablespoons low-sodium soy sauce
9¼ ounces diced, cooked chicken breast
2 tablespoons canola oil
2 cups green onions, thinly sliced
1 cup diced celery
2 cups canned crushed pineapple, packed in juice or light syrup
4 teaspoons sugar
4 teaspoons cornstarch

1. Make marinade: In a plastic bag, stir together 2 tablespoons water, soy sauce, and ¼ teaspoon each salt and pepper. Marinate chicken for 1 hour.
2. Heat 1 tablespoon of oil on medium–high in a medium stockpot. Sauté green onions and celery for 3–5 minutes until celery begins to cook, but stays crunchy. Remove vegetables, and set aside.
3. Add remaining 1 tablespoon oil to the pot. Add chicken, marinade, and pineapples with juice to pot. Continue cooking on medium–high heat, and bring to a boil, 5–7 minutes. Stir frequently.
4. Make cornstarch mixture: In a small bowl, whisk ¼ cup water together with sugar and cornstarch until smooth.
5. Stir cornstarch mixture into the chicken and pineapple. Bring to a boil. Reduce heat and cook for 3–5 minutes, or until sauce thickens. Stir frequently. Add 2 tablespoons of water if too thick.
6. Stir celery and green onions into pineapple chicken mixture, and cook for 1 minute.

Yield: 6 servings, ⅔ cup each
Meal Component: Meat/Meat Alternate, Fruit

Serving sizes are for ages 3–5. Guidelines for the proper credit of food may vary in some states. Please check with the CACFP in your state for more information.

Menu of the Month

Breakfast
Milk
Stone-Ground Grits (WG)
Mango Chunks

Morning Snack
Water
Baked Apples
Whole Grain Goldfish-Style Crackers (WG)

Lunch
Milk
Pineapple Chicken*
Brown Rice (WG)
Steamed Baby Bok Choi

Afternoon Snack
Water
Berry Nut Butter* (WG)

*Indicates recipes of the month.
(WG) Indicates whole grain
Pineapple Chicken recipe is adapted from the US Department of Agriculture.
Berry Nut Butter recipe is adapted from the Institute of Childhood Nutrition.

Berry Nut Butter

6 cups whole frozen strawberries, thawed and drained
6 tablespoons peanut butter, smooth
1½ cups whole grain-rich bear-shaped sweet crackers (at least 3 ounces total) or crushed graham crackers (at least 84 grams total)

1. In a medium bowl, combine strawberries and peanut butter. Use a hand or stand mixer to blend until smooth. Let sit for 10–15 minutes to settle.
2. Place ½ cup strawberry-peanut butter mixture each in six small bowls. Top with ¼ cup mini graham crackers (bear-shaped) or 14 grams crushed graham crackers.

Yield: 6 servings, one bowl each
Meal Component: Fruit, Meat/Meat Alternate, Grain

Nutrition and Fitness Notes

Adults are responsible for providing nutritious, appetizing food in an appropriate setting; children can decide how much or even whether they eat. Children generally eat only what pleases them on a specific day. Some children may eat only one or two food items, or eat a lot on one day and a little the next.

The Experienced Provider

Cultural responsiveness and inclusion require intentionality and constant engagement with children and families. Invite families to share their talents and expertise, showing children that their families are valued, and you recognize how proud children are of family members' knowledge. Families that can't physically come can tape a story for you to listen to during group gatherings or send a video showing how they make the family's favorite food.

Activities for Children

Learning about Families
A child does not exist in a silo. Ask children about their families, including pets, and keep notes. Send home an envelope containing small index cards, asking families to write the names of the significant people and/or pets in their child's life on each card. Put the cards onto a key ring, making a transitional object or a set of high-frequency words to support the writing of older children.

Reflecting the Ways We Live
Middle-class families are overwhelmingly represented in children's curricular materials, especially children's books. Early childhood educators can seek out books that discuss economic issues as well as books that feature settings familiar to some low-income children and their families. In addition to reading books, make a point of teaching infants and toddlers the vocabulary words for many types of homes and modes of transportation.

Implicit Bias
Implicit bias is difficult to see in ourselves. The good news is that it gets easier the more you use reflection. But identifying your biases is only the beginning. Addressing them is a lifelong process. The more you reflect on your own implicit bias, the less likely it is to affect your actions.

Literacy Corner

Who's in My Family? All about Our Families by Robie H. Harris
Learn about many different family configurations, each one "perfectly normal and totally wonderful," during a day at the zoo.

A Family Is a Family Is a Family by Sara O'Leary
One small girl learns about the different families in her class and discovers that the one quality they share is love.

DECEMBER ATTENDANCE AND PAYMENT LOG

To record drop-off and pickup times that vary, try using two lines per child.

CHILD'S NAME	S 1	M 2	T 3	W 4	T 5	F 6	S 7	TOTAL	S 8	M 9	T 10	W 11	T 12	F 13	S 14	TOTAL	S 15	M 16	T 17	W 18	T 19	F 20	S 21	TOTAL	S 22	M 23	T 24	W 25	T 26	F 27	S 28	TOTAL	S 29	M 30	T 31	W	T	F	S	TOTAL	S	M

DECEMBER ATTENDANCE AND PAYMENT LOG CONTINUED

CHILD'S NAME	S 1	M 2	T 3	W 4	T 5	F 6	S 7	TOTAL	S 8	M 9	T 10	W 11	T 12	F 13	S 14	TOTAL	S 15	M 16	T 17	W 18	T 19	F 20	S 21	TOTAL	S 22	M 23	T 24	W 25	T 26	F 27	S 28	TOTAL	S 29	M 30	T 31	W	T	F	S	TOTAL	S	M

WEEKLY PAYMENT TOTALS

	FOOD PROGRAM INCOME RECVD	PARENT FEE INCOME RECVD	OTHER INCOME RECVD			
DECEMBER INCOME				=	DEC TOTAL	
BALANCE FORWARD				=	BALANCE FWD TOTAL	
TOTAL Y-T-D INCOME				=	TOTAL Y-T-D	

Food Program Claim

Date Claim Sent _____

Date Check Received _____

MEAL COUNT TALLY

BREAKFASTS	
LUNCHES	
DINNERS	
SNACKS	

Put totals in year-end meal tally, page 95.

DECEMBER EXPENSE REPORT

DATE	PAYMENT TYPE cash, check #, cc #, debit	PURCHASED FROM	PURCHASE TOTAL	ADVERTISING	INSURANCE	INTEREST	LEGAL & PROFESSIONAL SERVICES	OFFICE EXPENSES (including internet & 2nd phone)	RENT OF BUSINESS PROPERTY	REPAIR & MAINTENANCE	SUPPLIES		MILES
		THIS MONTH'S TOTAL											
		BALANCE CARRIED FORWARD											
		YEAR-TO-DATE TOTAL											

DECEMBER EXPENSE REPORT

DATE	PAYMENT TYPE cash, check #, cc #, debit	PURCHASED FROM	PURCHASE TOTAL	TAXES & LICENSES	TRAVEL & ENTERTAINMENT	FOOD	TOYS	HOUSEHOLD ITEMS	CLEANING SUPPLIES	ACTIVITY EXPENSES			MILES
		THIS MONTH'S TOTAL											
		BALANCE CARRIED FORWARD											
		YEAR-TO-DATE TOTAL											

See page 85 for an explanation of how to transfer expenses to your tax forms. You may wish to relabel the columns to fit your business needs.

See page 6 for an explanation of the order in which we present the categories.

HOUSE EXPENSES WORKSHEET

YEAR:	Natural Gas		Electricity		Water/Sewer		Trash Collection		Cable TV	
	Date Paid	Amount	Date Paid	Amount	Date Paid	Amount	Date Paid	Amount	Date Paid	Amount
JANUARY										
FEBRUARY										
MARCH										
APRIL										
MAY										
JUNE										
JULY										
AUGUST										
SEPTEMBER										
OCTOBER										
NOVEMBER										
DECEMBER										
TOTAL										
TIME-SPACE PERCENTAGE										
FCC BUSINESS EXPENSE										

Homeowners Insurance		Property Taxes		Mortgage Interest or Rent		House Repairs & Maintenance	
Date Paid	Amount	Date Paid	Amount	Date Paid	Amount	Date Paid	Amount

NOTE: You are entitled to claim a portion of these house expenses for your business. Use this worksheet to record these expenses each month or once a year. For each column, fill in the total and your Time-Space percentage (to compute, see the *Family Child Care Record-Keeping Guide*, 9th edition). To arrive at the FCC business expense, multiply the total in each column by the Time-Space percentage.

Add together the FCC business expenses for natural gas, electricity, water/sewer, trash collection, and cable TV, and enter the total under Utilities on the next page. Take the totals of the other FCC business expense columns and enter them on the next page. When you file your taxes, the house expenses on this page go directly onto Form 8829 Expenses for Business Use of Your Home.

INCOME TAX WORKSHEET

TOTAL INCOME (See December Year-to-Date Total. Enter directly onto Form 1040 Schedule C.)	
EXPENSES	
I. DIRECT BUSINESS EXPENSES (See monthly expense reports. Enter directly onto Form 1040 Schedule C.)	
ADVERTISING	
CAR AND TRUCK EXPENSES (Include mileage and the business portion of any car-loan interest or excise tax.)	
LIABILITY INSURANCE	
BUSINESS INTEREST (not mortgage interest) (credit card interest on business portion of purchases)	
LEGAL AND PROFESSIONAL SERVICES	
OFFICE EXPENSES (postage, bank charges, education and training, dues, publications)	
RENT OF BUSINESS PROPERTY (other than home or apartment) (videos, carpet shampooer)	
REPAIRS AND MAINTENANCE OF PERSONAL PROPERTY (furniture, appliances, equipment)	
SUPPLIES	
TAXES AND LICENSES	
TRAVEL AND ENTERTAINMENT (for overnight conferences)	
FOOD (List under Other Expenses on Form 1040 Schedule C.)	
TOYS (List under Other Expenses on Form 1040 Schedule C.)	
HOUSEHOLD ITEMS, CLEANING SUPPLIES, AND ACTIVITY EXPENSES (List under Other Expenses on Form 1040 Schedule C.)	
II. HOUSE EXPENSES (See page 84. Enter directly onto Form 8829.)	
UTILITIES	
HOMEOWNERS INSURANCE	
PROPERTY TAXES	
MORTGAGE INTEREST OR RENT	
HOUSE REPAIRS AND MAINTENANCE (painting, broken glass)	
III. DEPRECIATION EXPENSES (Enter directly onto Form 8829 or Form 4562.)	
HOUSE (Form 8829)	
HOME IMPROVEMENTS (Form 4562) (new roof, furnace, remodeling)	
LAND IMPROVEMENTS (Form 4562 or Schedule C) (fence, driveway)	
TOTAL EXPENSES (deductions)	
NET INCOME (income minus expenses)	

How to Use This Worksheet

Use this worksheet at the end of the year to pull together all of your business expenses recorded on this *Redleaf Calendar-Keeper*. The categories of expenses listed here correspond to particular lines on the various tax forms that you must fill out for your business. Enter direct business expenses on Form 1040 Schedule C. Enter house expenses on Form 8829. Enter depreciation expenses on Form 8829 or Form 4562. After you have completed Forms 8829 and 4562, you will enter the totals from these forms onto your Schedule C.

You may wish to add or move some direct business expenses to different categories than are shown on this worksheet. Sometimes you may have two or more different expense categories on one receipt. You may either split the receipt and list items under more than one category or list all the expenses under one category. It doesn't matter which method you choose because all direct business expenses get totaled at the bottom of the Schedule C. You will not be penalized by the IRS for listing a supply expense under the food category or vice versa.

There are special rules concerning depreciation expenses. For a description of how to calculate depreciation expenses, see the *Family Child Care 2024 Tax Workbook and Organizer*.

PAYMENT AND INCOME RECORD FOR JANUARY–MARCH

CHILD'S NAME	JANUARY						JAN TOTAL	FEBRUARY						FEB TOTAL	MARCH						MAR TOTAL	1st Qtr* Total
SUBTOTALS																						
FOOD PROGRAM																						
OTHER INCOME																						
TOTALS																						

*1st quarter for estimated tax for the months of January–March. For income tax purposes, quarters are determined by the federal government and are not always the same as calendar quarters. Taxes for the 1st quarter are due April 15.

If you receive payments from a third party (such as a government agency) and don't get paid until a later month, use two lines per child and enter the payment date and check number on the second line.

PAYMENT AND INCOME RECORD FOR JANUARY–MARCH CONTINUED

CHILD'S NAME	JANUARY						JAN TOTAL	FEBRUARY						FEB TOTAL	MARCH						MAR TOTAL	1st Qtr* Total
SUBTOTALS																						
FOOD PROGRAM																						
OTHER INCOME																						
TOTALS																						

*1st quarter for estimated tax for the months of January–March. For income tax purposes, quarters are determined by the federal government and are not always the same as calendar quarters. Taxes for the 1st quarter are due April 15.

PAYMENT AND INCOME RECORD FOR APRIL–JUNE

CHILD'S NAME	APRIL						APR TOTAL	MAY						MAY TOTAL	2nd Qtr* TOTAL	JUNE						JUN TOTAL
SUBTOTALS																						
FOOD PROGRAM																						
OTHER INCOME																						
TOTALS																						

*2nd quarter for estimated tax for the months of April and May. For income tax purposes, quarters are determined by the federal government and are not always the same as calendar quarters. Taxes for the 2nd quarter are due June 17.

BALANCE CARRIED FORWARD

YEAR-TO-DATE TOTAL

PAYMENT AND INCOME RECORD FOR APRIL–JUNE CONTINUED

CHILD'S NAME	APRIL						APR TOTAL	MAY						MAY TOTAL	2nd Qtr* TOTAL	JUNE						JUN TOTAL
SUBTOTALS																						
FOOD PROGRAM																						
OTHER INCOME																						
TOTALS																						

BALANCE CARRIED FORWARD

YEAR-TO-DATE TOTAL

*2nd quarter for estimated tax for the months of April and May. For income tax purposes, quarters are determined by the federal government and are not always the same as calendar quarters. Taxes for the 2nd quarter are due June 17.

PAYMENT AND INCOME RECORD FOR JULY–SEPTEMBER

CHILD'S NAME	JULY						JUL TOTAL	AUGUST						AUG TOTAL	3rd Qtr* TOTAL	SEPTEMBER						SEP TOTAL
SUBTOTALS																						
FOOD PROGRAM																						
OTHER INCOME																						
TOTALS																						

*3rd quarter for estimated tax for the months of June–August. For income tax purposes, quarters are determined by the federal government and are not always the same as calendar quarters. Taxes for the 3rd quarter are due September 16.

BALANCE CARRIED FORWARD

YEAR-TO-DATE TOTAL

PAYMENT AND INCOME RECORD FOR JULY–SEPTEMBER CONTINUED

CHILD'S NAME	JULY						JUL TOTAL	AUGUST							AUG TOTAL	3rd Qtr* TOTAL	SEPTEMBER						SEP TOTAL
SUBTOTALS																							
FOOD PROGRAM																							
OTHER INCOME																							
TOTALS																							

BALANCE CARRIED FORWARD

YEAR-TO-DATE TOTAL

*3rd quarter for estimated tax for the months of June–August. For income tax purposes, quarters are determined by the federal government and are not always the same as calendar quarters. Taxes for the 3rd quarter are due September 16.

PAYMENT AND INCOME RECORD FOR OCTOBER–DECEMBER

CHILD'S NAME	OCTOBER						OCT TOTAL	NOVEMBER						NOV TOTAL	DECEMBER						DEC TOTAL	4th Qtr* TOTAL
SUBTOTALS																						
FOOD PROGRAM																						
OTHER INCOME																						
TOTALS																						

*4th quarter for estimated tax for the months of September–December. For income tax purposes, quarters are determined by the federal government and are not always the same as calendar quarters. Taxes for the 4th quarter are due January 15, 2025.

Income should be reported as income in the year you receive it, not the year you earn it. Payments received after December 31, 2023, for child care services you delivered in 2023 should be reported as income in 2024.

BALANCE CARRIED FORWARD

2024 TOTAL

PAYMENT AND INCOME RECORD FOR OCTOBER–DECEMBER CONTINUED

CHILD'S NAME	OCTOBER						OCT TOTAL	NOVEMBER						NOV TOTAL	DECEMBER						DEC TOTAL	4th Qtr* TOTAL
SUBTOTALS																						
FOOD PROGRAM																						
OTHER INCOME																						
TOTALS																						

*4th quarter for estimated tax for the months of September–December. For income tax purposes, quarters are determined by the federal government and are not always the same as calendar quarters. Taxes for the 4th quarter are due January 15, 2025.

Income should be reported as income in the year you receive it, not the year you earn it. Payments received after December 31, 2023, for child care services you delivered in 2023 should be reported as income in 2024.

BALANCE CARRIED FORWARD

2024 TOTAL

MEAL FORM Week of _____ 2024

Child	Mon	Tue	Wed	Thu	Fri	Sat	Sun	Totals	Child	Mon	Tue	Wed	Thu	Fri	Sat	Sun	Totals
	Bkst ___ Lun ___ Din ___ Sn1 ___ Sn2 ___ Sn3 ___	Bkst ___ Lun ___ Din ___ Sn1 ___ Sn2 ___ Sn3 ___	Bkst ___ Lun ___ Din ___ Sn1 ___ Sn2 ___ Sn3 ___	Bkst ___ Lun ___ Din ___ Sn1 ___ Sn2 ___ Sn3 ___	Bkst ___ Lun ___ Din ___ Sn1 ___ Sn2 ___ Sn3 ___	Bkst ___ Lun ___ Din ___ Sn1 ___ Sn2 ___ Sn3 ___	Bkst ___ Lun ___ Din ___ Sn1 ___ Sn2 ___ Sn3 ___	B ___ L ___ D ___ S ___		Bkst ___ Lun ___ Din ___ Sn1 ___ Sn2 ___ Sn3 ___	Bkst ___ Lun ___ Din ___ Sn1 ___ Sn2 ___ Sn3 ___	Bkst ___ Lun ___ Din ___ Sn1 ___ Sn2 ___ Sn3 ___	Bkst ___ Lun ___ Din ___ Sn1 ___ Sn2 ___ Sn3 ___	Bkst ___ Lun ___ Din ___ Sn1 ___ Sn2 ___ Sn3 ___	Bkst ___ Lun ___ Din ___ Sn1 ___ Sn2 ___ Sn3 ___	Bkst ___ Lun ___ Din ___ Sn1 ___ Sn2 ___ Sn3 ___	B ___ L ___ D ___ S ___
	Bkst ___ Lun ___ Din ___ Sn1 ___ Sn2 ___ Sn3 ___	Bkst ___ Lun ___ Din ___ Sn1 ___ Sn2 ___ Sn3 ___	Bkst ___ Lun ___ Din ___ Sn1 ___ Sn2 ___ Sn3 ___	Bkst ___ Lun ___ Din ___ Sn1 ___ Sn2 ___ Sn3 ___	Bkst ___ Lun ___ Din ___ Sn1 ___ Sn2 ___ Sn3 ___	Bkst ___ Lun ___ Din ___ Sn1 ___ Sn2 ___ Sn3 ___	Bkst ___ Lun ___ Din ___ Sn1 ___ Sn2 ___ Sn3 ___	B ___ L ___ D ___ S ___		Bkst ___ Lun ___ Din ___ Sn1 ___ Sn2 ___ Sn3 ___	Bkst ___ Lun ___ Din ___ Sn1 ___ Sn2 ___ Sn3 ___	Bkst ___ Lun ___ Din ___ Sn1 ___ Sn2 ___ Sn3 ___	Bkst ___ Lun ___ Din ___ Sn1 ___ Sn2 ___ Sn3 ___	Bkst ___ Lun ___ Din ___ Sn1 ___ Sn2 ___ Sn3 ___	Bkst ___ Lun ___ Din ___ Sn1 ___ Sn2 ___ Sn3 ___	Bkst ___ Lun ___ Din ___ Sn1 ___ Sn2 ___ Sn3 ___	B ___ L ___ D ___ S ___
	Bkst ___ Lun ___ Din ___ Sn1 ___ Sn2 ___ Sn3 ___	Bkst ___ Lun ___ Din ___ Sn1 ___ Sn2 ___ Sn3 ___	Bkst ___ Lun ___ Din ___ Sn1 ___ Sn2 ___ Sn3 ___	Bkst ___ Lun ___ Din ___ Sn1 ___ Sn2 ___ Sn3 ___	Bkst ___ Lun ___ Din ___ Sn1 ___ Sn2 ___ Sn3 ___	Bkst ___ Lun ___ Din ___ Sn1 ___ Sn2 ___ Sn3 ___	Bkst ___ Lun ___ Din ___ Sn1 ___ Sn2 ___ Sn3 ___	B ___ L ___ D ___ S ___		Bkst ___ Lun ___ Din ___ Sn1 ___ Sn2 ___ Sn3 ___	Bkst ___ Lun ___ Din ___ Sn1 ___ Sn2 ___ Sn3 ___	Bkst ___ Lun ___ Din ___ Sn1 ___ Sn2 ___ Sn3 ___	Bkst ___ Lun ___ Din ___ Sn1 ___ Sn2 ___ Sn3 ___	Bkst ___ Lun ___ Din ___ Sn1 ___ Sn2 ___ Sn3 ___	Bkst ___ Lun ___ Din ___ Sn1 ___ Sn2 ___ Sn3 ___	Bkst ___ Lun ___ Din ___ Sn1 ___ Sn2 ___ Sn3 ___	B ___ L ___ D ___ S ___
	Bkst ___ Lun ___ Din ___ Sn1 ___ Sn2 ___ Sn3 ___	Bkst ___ Lun ___ Din ___ Sn1 ___ Sn2 ___ Sn3 ___	Bkst ___ Lun ___ Din ___ Sn1 ___ Sn2 ___ Sn3 ___	Bkst ___ Lun ___ Din ___ Sn1 ___ Sn2 ___ Sn3 ___	Bkst ___ Lun ___ Din ___ Sn1 ___ Sn2 ___ Sn3 ___	Bkst ___ Lun ___ Din ___ Sn1 ___ Sn2 ___ Sn3 ___	Bkst ___ Lun ___ Din ___ Sn1 ___ Sn2 ___ Sn3 ___	B ___ L ___ D ___ S ___		Bkst ___ Lun ___ Din ___ Sn1 ___ Sn2 ___ Sn3 ___	Bkst ___ Lun ___ Din ___ Sn1 ___ Sn2 ___ Sn3 ___	Bkst ___ Lun ___ Din ___ Sn1 ___ Sn2 ___ Sn3 ___	Bkst ___ Lun ___ Din ___ Sn1 ___ Sn2 ___ Sn3 ___	Bkst ___ Lun ___ Din ___ Sn1 ___ Sn2 ___ Sn3 ___	Bkst ___ Lun ___ Din ___ Sn1 ___ Sn2 ___ Sn3 ___	Bkst ___ Lun ___ Din ___ Sn1 ___ Sn2 ___ Sn3 ___	B ___ L ___ D ___ S ___
	Bkst ___ Lun ___ Din ___ Sn1 ___ Sn2 ___ Sn3 ___	Bkst ___ Lun ___ Din ___ Sn1 ___ Sn2 ___ Sn3 ___	Bkst ___ Lun ___ Din ___ Sn1 ___ Sn2 ___ Sn3 ___	Bkst ___ Lun ___ Din ___ Sn1 ___ Sn2 ___ Sn3 ___	Bkst ___ Lun ___ Din ___ Sn1 ___ Sn2 ___ Sn3 ___	Bkst ___ Lun ___ Din ___ Sn1 ___ Sn2 ___ Sn3 ___	Bkst ___ Lun ___ Din ___ Sn1 ___ Sn2 ___ Sn3 ___	B ___ L ___ D ___ S ___		Bkst ___ Lun ___ Din ___ Sn1 ___ Sn2 ___ Sn3 ___	Bkst ___ Lun ___ Din ___ Sn1 ___ Sn2 ___ Sn3 ___	Bkst ___ Lun ___ Din ___ Sn1 ___ Sn2 ___ Sn3 ___	Bkst ___ Lun ___ Din ___ Sn1 ___ Sn2 ___ Sn3 ___	Bkst ___ Lun ___ Din ___ Sn1 ___ Sn2 ___ Sn3 ___	Bkst ___ Lun ___ Din ___ Sn1 ___ Sn2 ___ Sn3 ___	Bkst ___ Lun ___ Din ___ Sn1 ___ Sn2 ___ Sn3 ___	B ___ L ___ D ___ S ___
	Bkst ___ Lun ___ Din ___ Sn1 ___ Sn2 ___ Sn3 ___	Bkst ___ Lun ___ Din ___ Sn1 ___ Sn2 ___ Sn3 ___	Bkst ___ Lun ___ Din ___ Sn1 ___ Sn2 ___ Sn3 ___	Bkst ___ Lun ___ Din ___ Sn1 ___ Sn2 ___ Sn3 ___	Bkst ___ Lun ___ Din ___ Sn1 ___ Sn2 ___ Sn3 ___	Bkst ___ Lun ___ Din ___ Sn1 ___ Sn2 ___ Sn3 ___	Bkst ___ Lun ___ Din ___ Sn1 ___ Sn2 ___ Sn3 ___	B ___ L ___ D ___ S ___		Bkst ___ Lun ___ Din ___ Sn1 ___ Sn2 ___ Sn3 ___	Bkst ___ Lun ___ Din ___ Sn1 ___ Sn2 ___ Sn3 ___	Bkst ___ Lun ___ Din ___ Sn1 ___ Sn2 ___ Sn3 ___	Bkst ___ Lun ___ Din ___ Sn1 ___ Sn2 ___ Sn3 ___	Bkst ___ Lun ___ Din ___ Sn1 ___ Sn2 ___ Sn3 ___	Bkst ___ Lun ___ Din ___ Sn1 ___ Sn2 ___ Sn3 ___	Bkst ___ Lun ___ Din ___ Sn1 ___ Sn2 ___ Sn3 ___	B ___ L ___ D ___ S ___

Place a check mark (✓) next to each meal or snack you serve. Do not count meals served to your own children. If you are on the Food Program, use this form to track your nonreimbursed meals only. Add the reimbursed meals from your monthly claim forms and the nonreimbursed meals from this form together, and put the totals on the year-end meal tally on page 95. If you are not on the Food Program, use this form to track all your meals, and put the totals on the year-end meal tally on page 95.

Make copies of this form for each week of the year. If you have six or fewer children in your program, you can use one form for two weeks. You can download this form at the Redleaf Press website. Go to www.redleafpress.org, and find the page for the *Redleaf Calendar-Keeper 2024*. There will be a link to this form.

Weekly Totals

Breakfasts _____   Dinners _____

Lunches _____   Snacks _____

YEAR-END MEAL TALLY

If you are not on the Food Program, enter all meals and snacks in the column labeled "Number Not Reimbursed by Food Program."

	Breakfasts		Lunches		Dinners		Snacks	
	Number Reimbursed by Food Program	Number Not Reimbursed by Food Program	Number Reimbursed by Food Program	Number Not Reimbursed by Food Program	Number Reimbursed by Food Program	Number Not Reimbursed by Food Program	Number Reimbursed by Food Program	Number Not Reimbursed by Food Program
January								
February								
March								
April								
May								
June								
July								
August								
September								
October								
November								
December								
TOTAL								

2024 Standard Meal Allowance Rate*

Number of Breakfasts _____ X $1.65 = $_____
Number of Lunches _____ X $3.12 = $_____
Number of Dinners _____ X $3.12 = $_____
Number of Snacks _____ X $0.93 = $_____
Total Food Deductions $_____ †

Do not report any meals served to your own children (even if they are reimbursed by the Food Program).

* The IRS standard meal allowance rate for 2024 used in these calculations is based on the Tier I rate as of January 1, 2024. This rate is used for all meals and snacks served throughout 2024, even though the Tier I rate goes up every July. All providers, whether on Tier I or Tier II (and all providers not on the Food Program), will use the rates listed.

† Enter this amount on Form 1040 Schedule C, Part V. Be sure to enter any reimbursements from the Food Program (with the exception of reimbursements for your own children) as income on Form 1040 Schedule C, line 6.

EMERGENCY PHONE NUMBERS

PROVIDER'S ADDRESS	FIRE	POLICE
	EMERGENCY SQUAD	POISON CONTROL CENTER
PROVIDER'S PHONE #	LOCAL HOSPITAL	OTHER

IN EMERGENCIES USE 911 IF AVAILABLE

Child's Name	Birth Date	Parent / Guardian		Parent / Guardian		Emergency Contact		Doctor	
		Name / Home #	Work # / Cell #	Name / Home #	Work # / Cell #	Name	Phone #	Name	Phone #

EMERGENCY PHONE NUMBERS (continued from page 96)

Child's Name	Birth Date	Parent / Guardian		Parent / Guardian		Emergency Contact		Doctor	
		Name / Home #	Work # / Cell #	Name / Home #	Work # / Cell #	Name	Phone #	Name	Phone #

WAITING LIST

Child's Name	Age	Parent/Guardian Names	Phone #	Date of Call	Date Needed
			W H W H		
			W H W H		
			W H W H		
			W H W H		
			W H W H		
			W H W H		
			W H W H		
			W H W H		
			W H W H		

EMERGENCY DRILL RECORD

	Time/Date	No. and Ages of Children	Type of Drill	Evac. Time
JAN			Fire	
FEB			Fire	
MAR			Fire	
APR			Fire	
MAY			Fire	
JUN			Fire	
JUL			Fire	
AUG			Fire	
SEP			Fire	
OCT			Fire	
NOV			Fire	
DEC			Fire	